# IMPERFECT
# PRESIDENTS

# IMPERFECT PRESIDENTS

✶✶✶✶✶✶✶✶✶✶✶✶✶✶✶✶✶✶✶✶✶✶✶✶✶✶✶✶✶✶✶✶✶✶✶✶✶✶✶✶✶✶✶✶✶

## TALES OF MISADVENTURE AND TRIUMPH

✶✶✶✶✶✶✶✶✶✶✶✶✶✶✶✶✶✶✶✶✶✶✶✶✶✶✶✶✶✶✶✶✶✶✶✶✶✶✶✶✶✶✶✶✶

## JIM CULLEN

FALL RIVER PRESS

Fall River Press
122 Fifth Avenue
New York, NY 10011

ISBN: 978-1-4351-2384-7

Printed and bound in the United States of America

10  9  8  7  6  5  4  3  2  1

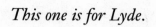

*This one is for Lyde.*

*The law will never make men free;*
*it is men who have got to make the law free.*
—Henry David Thoreau,
"Slavery in Massachusetts," 1854

# CONTENTS

# ACKNOWLEDGMENTS

*A*lice Martell: My first words of thanks. Every writer has the fantasy of the unexpected benefactor, a highly credible figure who emerges from the mists and tells you you're good (as good as you sometimes believe you are, better than the fraud you know yourself to be). More than that: This person actually makes things happen, things you could never do for yourself. Alice swept into my life in the spring of 2005, made me presentable, shopped me around, sold my work, checked up on me periodically to see how I was doing, forgave my missteps, and—given some of my previous experience with agents, I still can't quite get over this—returned my phone calls. The word that describes my dazed gratitude is "marvel." I don't really deserve such treatment. The Puritans called it irresistible grace. The Lord works in mysterious ways, and I'm here to tell you that one of those ways is Alice.

She didn't do it alone. Another agent of my good fortune is my editor, Alessandra Bastagli. This was not supposed to be a book on the presidency. Actually, it began as a website on flawed but admirable Americans called *American History for Cynical Beginners.*\* But Alessandra had the vision and the skill to help me focus it into a more svelte narrative form, and much of any merit this project has is attributable to her. I'd also like to thank other members of the Palgrave team: copyeditor Rick Delaney, who read the manuscript with skill and care; associate production editor Yasmin Mathew, who shepherded me through the production process,

---

\* You can see it for yourself: www.ecfs.org/projects/jcullen

and Letra Libre, who designed the book. Special thanks as well to marketing manager Amy Tiedemann, Lauren Dwyer, and the editorial director of Palgrave, Airié Stuart.

Since coming to the Ethical Culture Fieldston School in 2001, I have benefited from the company and counsel of a cherished array of students and colleagues, some of whom allowed me to run road tests of this material by them. I am also thankful to the librarians of the Tate Library at Fieldston—Nelie Locher, Mandy Colgan, and Carol Oreskovic—who chased down leads, ordered books, and provided the kind of cheerful competence that is the special province of their breed. The Venture Grant board at ECFS provided crucial seeding in funding the website, and Associate Head of School Beth Beckmann channeled some institutional largesse in my direction as well. I am grateful to these people as well as to the head of the school, Joe Healey, for their administrative support and goodwill.

This book was wedged into an everyday life that I think could be legitimately regarded as busy. My four children accepted their father's distraction without entirely understanding it. My wife, to whom this book is dedicated, tolerated her husband's distraction despite understanding it all too well. It is a strange conceit to think that anything one might say to a stranger could be as valuable as that which one does with a loved one. I have indulged what sometimes seemed like a literal itch to write by scratching a metaphorical pen. I hope none of us—and that includes you, dear reader—are worse for it.

*—Jim Cullen*
*Hastings-on-Hudson, New York*
*November, 2006*

# IMPERFECT PRESIDENTS

# THE PRESIDENT WE WANT

For most of us, for most of the time, it doesn't really matter who the President of the United States is. We get up in the morning, go to school or work, see our friends and families, balance our checkbooks (or try to, anyway), eat our meals, sleep in our beds. We have our passions, our struggles, our aspirations. And every once in a while, we may stop to realize that the very fact of it not mattering is part of what makes us lucky to be Americans. It's one of the forms our freedom takes: the freedom not to care.

Even for most of the people who work for the federal government, it doesn't matter who the President of the United States is. Members of the U.S. Congress and Supreme Court have responsibilities and concerns completely separate from those of the executive branch, as do state and local government officers. Moreover, a vast army of appointed officials watch politicians come and go, their own work largely invisible—and stubbornly resistant to change—no matter who happens to live at 1600 Pennsylvania Avenue.

Yet however irrelevant he may be—and we have been invariably talking about a "he" so far—the President of the United States is also an inescapable presence in our daily lives. Whether we want to or not, we see him in the morning when we watch TV, surf the web, or open a newspaper, and we hear about him over dinner or in the employee lounge. We're told endless details about his friends, his family, his foibles, and we hear jokes about him. Every four years we have a presidential election, and long before most of us would care to think about it, we're bombarded with ads, and with armchair speculating and strategizing over scenarios that never come to pass.

Presidents also sometimes become a kind of social shorthand for measuring and characterizing a time. The "Age of Eisenhower," for example, conjures up a series of time-specific images: new suburban homes and highways; television shows like *The Adventures of Ozzie and Harriet* and *I Love Lucy;* highballs and martinis; men in gray flannel suits and women in poodle skirts; and so on. Of course that very moment was also one of anxieties over juvenile delinquency, the emergence of the Civil Rights movement, and a "problem with no name" that launched the modern feminist movement—all of which were largely tangential to the Eisenhower administration. And yet the very significance, even intensity, of these latter phenomena were defined against a mainstream that Eisenhower—the twice-elected, highly popular, and reassuringly conventional president—represented.

Indeed, the perceived personality of a president is almost always more important than specific policies he advocates. True, most chief executives are representatives of political parties that seek to advance a general political philosophy (one usually related, in one form or another, to a belief in the proper scope of the federal government). But the reception of specific decisions a president makes are usually filtered through a more durable, and usually decisive, lens of personality. Franklin Delano Roosevelt's popularity was not directly correlated with his policies—it could not have been, because his actions in office directly contradicted promises he made (like balancing the federal budget during the 1932 presidential campaign, or keeping the United States out of World War II in 1940) without any negative impact on his political effectiveness. Instead, it is generally agreed, it was Roosevelt's indomitable spirit of optimism that voters responded to, a mood he projected that proved far more important than logically curious assertions (like "we have nothing to fear but fear itself") or policies that were in fact deeply unpopular (like trying to pack the Supreme Court with pliable appointees). Insofar as specific actions matter—like those of Richard Nixon between the Watergate break-in of June 1972 and his resignation a little over two years later—it's because such actions lead Americans to revise their overall perception of a president's character. Nixon felt compelled to say "I am not a crook" in 1973 precisely because that's what most Americans concluded he was, even before all the corroborating evidence was in.

The correlation between a president's character and the situations in which he finds himself can be complicated to untangle. Andrew Jackson seemed to place his imprint on his era by sheer force of personality; Jimmy Carter seemed buffeted by events beyond his control—and was viewed as ineffectual for precisely this reason. Though presidents are in office for a tiny fraction of their lives, it's that fraction that permanently defines their public personae, even when they had substantial lives before entering and after leaving office.

The two parts of that equation—the "numerator" of holding office and "denominator" that marks the rest of a president's life—form the key quotient of a presidential character. Typically those two pieces point toward a whole; voters pretty much knew what they were getting when they elected Calvin Coolidge president in 1924 (a terse, minimalist leadership style, epitomized by the way he broke a police strike as the governor of Massachusetts), and he pretty much fulfilled those expectations in the Oval Office. Occasionally, there was a big divergence. Ulysses S. Grant saved the Union as a decisive military leader during the Civil War, but in his eight years as president between 1869 and 1877 he passively condoned widespread corruption and marred his stellar reputation. The element of unpredictability is what makes presidential politics both intriguing and frustrating.

All presidents make mistakes. They're human. We all know that, and yet many of us have trouble fully accepting this truth. In part, that's a function of the presidency itself, which fuses the head of the government and the head of the state into a single person. The British feel free to jeer at the prime minister right to his face in the House of Commons; jeering at the Queen is another matter. From the moment he is elected, the president is endowed with an otherworldly aura, even by friends on a first-name basis who now refer to him as "Mr. President." And from the moment he is elected he becomes fodder for late-night comedians, and begins the inevitable process of disappointing at least some of the people all of the time. Meanwhile, there are those who think of politics as a four-letter word; election to the presidency is in itself proof that a candidate has cut a deal with the devil. No president has been immune from such carping and suspicion.

There is much to be gained from an attempt to see presidents whole, to appreciate their strengths as well as their weaknesses—and, perhaps more importantly, to appreciate those strengths in light of their weaknesses. Given the sheer scope of the challenges involved in becoming president, it is safe to say that anyone who has ever held the job exhibits traits that would be worth emulating. And given the fallibility of human beings generally, and the kinds of vices to which a president is particularly susceptible, it also seems reasonable that every president offers a cautionary tale. The lessons these people afford are illuminating in the context of American politics, to be sure. But in embodying tendencies of Americans in a particular time and place, they open a window on the American character generally—who we are, who we're not, and who we may yet be.

The stories that comprise this book all begin the same way: A man in a moment of weakness or confusion, acting in ways few of us would regard as appropriate. John Quincy Adams refusing to attend his successor's inauguration. Theodore Roosevelt making an absurdly pretentious entrance into the New York State Assembly. Gerald Ford attending a meeting of questionable propriety about Richard Nixon. Far from random miscalculation, however, the actions of these people reflect important aspects of their characters—they represent a kind of honesty. Moreover, the same character traits that get them into trouble are also manifestations of an inner strength that ultimately serves the country well. So, for example, Chester Alan Arthur violated a cardinal rule of politics by forsaking loyalty to his cronies, but when he unexpectedly landed in the White House he realized he had a higher loyalty to the American people. It is also true, however, that the presidential triumph in each of these cases has sometimes come from a decision (typically temporary) to consciously act against type. Thomas

Jefferson, for instance, was able to consummate the most successful act of his presidency only by actively resisting powerful philosophical inclinations. At other times, success is simultaneously an
affirmation and a refutation of a particular trait. Ronald Reagan's
behavior toward the Soviet Union in his second term was both a
reversal of his career-long hostility to that nation as well as the
fulfillment of an overriding desire—one that had gotten him into
some serious trouble—to bring the Cold War to a decisive close.

Some of the figures examined here are widely considered
great, like Lincoln and the two Roosevelts. Others, like Arthur
and Adams, are obscure to most Americans today. Still others,
like Lyndon Johnson and Bill Clinton, remain deeply controversial. Five of the subjects here are Republicans, three are Democrats, and two were president before the advent of the modern
party system. Many of the misadventures described here take
place before the man in question became president, followed by a
particular success in office. But sometimes both halves of the
story occur in the White House, and in one case (Adams) both
occur afterward. Even old men make foolish mistakes—and tran-
scend them.

The core conviction animating this book is a belief that, like
choosing a spouse, choosing the president we want is an affair of
the heart no less than one of the head. To understand your president, however imperfectly, is, however imperfectly, to understand yourself.

*(previous page)* TIME OF TRIAL: *The Prayer at Valley Forge*, painted by H. Brueckner; engraved by John C. McRae, 1866. Most portraits of Washington depict him with Olympian detachment. But there were crucial moments in the Revolution—Valley Forge was one; the Newburgh Conspiracy was another—where the cause was in doubt and Washington's leadership in question. (Presidential Portraits, Library of Congress)

# GENERAL WASHINGTON CODDLES A PROTÉGÉ

*In which we see a winter soldier demon-strate the limits of power, the power of limits, and a new kind of leadership in a new kind of nation.*

It is early March, 1783. After almost eight years of armed struggle, an insurgent army on the North American continent is on the cusp of victory against the global empire of Great Britain. Now, with the rebel military under the command of General George Washington headquartered in Newburgh, New York, 70 miles up the Hudson River from British-occupied Manhattan, American soldiers wait, encamped, for word on the peace negotiations taking place in Paris.

Despite the fact that victory is at hand, all is not well in this army. Junior officers in particular are restless. They're actually afraid of peace, because they think it means they're going to get shafted—again. Ever since they joined the army, the divided and often chaotic Continental Congress has provided them with constant misery: poor or insufficient supplies, little or no pay, and a string of broken promises. If the war ends now, the officers fear that Congress will have no incentive to address these issues. It will simply send everyone home, impoverished, to face families that have themselves endured years of hardship. This, apparently, is what "freedom" is going to mean.

It's widely known that members of the Continental Congress are disgusted with each other, for reasons that have little to do with the army. Wealthy contractors and bankers who have not been paid what they're owed by the government are also upset with the Congress. Rumor has it that congressional leaders have been talking with a small group of officers, who are planning to take matters into their own hands. They will force the government to do the right thing—whatever it takes. The whispering in Newburgh suggests that the call to action will come any day now.

The key question is what the man in charge will do. Three weeks earlier, on February 13, 1783, Alexander Hamilton, a former aide to General Washington, now a representative in Congress, wrote an exquisitely calibrated letter to his mentor that managed to both invite and sidestep treason. We all know, Hamilton told Washington, that the situation is potentially explosive, and despite what all responsible people may want, it could quickly get out of hand. The challenge will be "to keep a *complaining* and *suffering army* within the bounds of moderation."

This, Hamilton told the commander-in-chief, is where you come in.

> It will be advisable not to discountenance their endeavours to procure redress, but rather by the intervention of confidential and prudent persons, *to take direction of them*. This however must not appear: it is of moment to the public tranquility that Your Excellency should preserve the confidence of the army without losing that of the people. This will enable you in case of extremity to guide the torrent, and bring order[,] perhaps even good, out of confusion.[1]

Translation: Overthrow the government? Of course not! But it would not be a bad idea to covertly take the lead once the insurrection gets underway.

It's not known exactly when Hamilton's letter reached Washington (it probably would have taken a week to reach Newburgh from Philadelphia). But for reasons that remain unclear—perhaps he didn't regard the situation as urgent, or perhaps he wanted to strike just the right tone—Washington failed to respond for weeks, weeks in which the festering resentments were building toward a climax. When he finally did respond, on March 4, he adopted a mild tone that belied the tension that surrounded him. Washington was aware of that tension; it kept him in Newburgh rather than taking a well-earned leave. Despite this agitation, and despite the deeply subversive subtext of his protégé's letter—a protégé toward whom Washington consistently showed more patience than many of his contemporaries would have liked—the tone of his reply was relatively calm (though he did close by saying that their exchange was, and should remain, private). While he agreed with Hamilton that the situation with the army was indeed serious, Washington reported that, "I shall pursue the same steady line of conduct which has governed me hitherto." For all the whispering going on, he asserted he was under "no *great* apprehension" that anything big was about to happen.[2]

He was wrong. Something big was already underway.

The opening battles of the American Revolution had been fought on the colonial side by local militias, like the legendary "Minutemen," so named because they were ready to fight at a moment's notice. Such organizations could be effective in localized combat precisely because their members were volunteers who were fighting for their homes. Yet for this very reason, they were reluctant to travel very far—and, especially, to submit to control by outsiders. Americans of the thirteen colonies were going to need a standing professional army if they were going to win their independence as a group. "To place any dependence upon militia is, assuredly, resting upon a broken staff," Washington asserted in 1776.[3] Only an organization of paid soldiers contractually committed for the long haul (such as a three-year enlistment) was likely to stand up to the British in a sustained way. "The summer soldier and sunshine patriot" would be insufficient, Thomas Paine warned the colonists in his first issue of *The Crisis*, a series of essays he wrote in support of the cause.[4]

The problem was that the suspicious and financially strapped colonies were often grudging about giving the army the resources necessary to wage, never mind win, the war. The result was vividly on display in the winter of 1777–78, when the Continental Army wintered at Valley Forge, Pennsylvania. A sick, hungry, cold, and half-naked collection of men tottered on the edge of destruction.

Amid this mix of desperation and patriotism were financial incentives that also fueled the Continental Army. A typical volunteer received a $10 bonus upon enlistment (with a salary that varied depending on rank) and a promise of 100 acres of land upon the completion of his service. In 1780, Congress sweetened the offer for officers in particular by promising them they would receive pensions at half-salary in recognition of their service.

Commanding these troops would be no simple task. John Adams of Massachusetts nominated Washington—who as a young colonial officer bungled a mission in the Virginia backwoods, triggering the worldwide Seven Years' War in 1754—because he was one of the few revolutionaries with any military experience, and because Adams thought it was symbolically important that a Southerner lead what in 1775 were mostly New England troops. Yet Adams was also skeptical of Washington for much of the war because he feared the despotic potential of any man with that much power. And Adams was not alone.

In an important sense, however, the biggest challenge Washington faced wasn't in getting too little respect, but too much. In the spring of 1782, with tensions mounting in the Continental Army over the state of the army and congressional gridlock, one of his officers wrote him suggesting that "strong arguments might be produced for admitting the title of king," and that there had been some conversation about crowning him king. Washington responded by saying, "no occurrence in the War has given me more painful sensations than your information of there being such ideas existing in the Army."[5] Washington, a

committed republican, had no interest in becoming George I—
as far as he was concerned, this was a negation of everything the
Revolution was about.

Washington may have wished that such talk would go away,
but he seemed fully aware it was intensifying in the months that
followed. His correspondence with Congress in 1782–83 was an
anxious stream of complaints, demands, and laments about the
lack of resources for his men. Despite the lack of action after
the climactic Battle of Yorktown in October 1781, Washington
declined to take time off and visit his family because, as he
wrote Secretary of War Benjamin Lincoln, he felt he needed to
be "like a careful physician to prevent if possible the disorders
getting to an incurable height." By December, he was writing
Virginia Congressman Joseph Jones, saying, "the temper of the
Army is much soured, and has become more irritable than at
any time since the commencement of the War." In early 1783,
Jones himself wrote back that "reports are freely circulated here
that there are dangerous combinations in the army" and that
some of the conspirators were even trying to blacken Washington's reputation.[6]

These reports were rooted in reality. Unpaid for months,
there was widespread doubt among officers that they would ever
see their pensions, and they began setting their sights on getting
a lump-sum payment now rather than hoping for more later. In
December of 1782, a group of officers at the army's headquarters in Newburgh sent a delegation to the national capital at
Philadelphia to make such a deal. "We have borne all that men
can bear—our property is expended—our private resources are
at an end, and our friends are wearied out and disgusted with
our incessant applications," their petition read. "Any further ex-
periments on their patience may have fatal effects."[7] This was a
vague but unmistakable threat that the army might take matters
into its own hands.

There were some in Congress who were sympathetic to this
delegation and willing to act on its behalf. Under the leadership
of these men, who included Hamilton of New York and James
Madison of Virginia, a proposal was made in January 1783
whereby the colonies would agree to tax imports in order to pay

the army as well as government creditors. The Newburgh delegation testified that Congress could expect "at least mutiny" if the army wasn't satisfied, and the nation's finance minister, Roger Morris, resigned to impress upon wavering congressmen just how serious the state of the nation's finances were.[8] Despite the high-pressure tactics, however, the proposal failed, leaving matters unresolved.

The crisis intensified the following month, when, on February 13, news arrived in Philadelphia that preliminary articles of peace had been signed in Paris between Britain and the new United States of America. Those who wanted to force Congress to address the army/creditor problem concluded it was now or never. An emissary from Philadelphia headed back to Newburgh with instructions for a group of conspirators there. And Hamilton dispatched his highly disingenuous letter to Washington, suggesting now might be the time for him to seize leadership of the insurrection. But Washington, for all his evident anxiety, remained passive. Delaying in his reply to Hamilton, he continued to hang back in the days that followed.

Events at headquarters forced his hand. On Monday, March 10, amid rumors the army would join with public creditors to move on Philadelphia, where even many members of Congress would welcome an army takeover, an unsigned manifesto began circulating at army headquarters. This first "Newburgh Address," as it has come to be known, exhorted officers to reject "the meek language of entreating memorials" and "change the milk-and-water style" of their correspondence with Congress. If the war was indeed over, then no one should surrender his arms until his grievances had been met. And if the war wasn't over, they should "retire to some unsettled country, smile in your turn, and 'mock when their fear cometh on.'"[9]

The vigilant but minimalist approach the commander-in-chief had adopted for the past year-and-a-half no longer seemed adequate: If he didn't do something now, the ship would sail without him. Now Washington acted with striking speed—and his first move was to freeze the conspiracy in its tracks. On Tuesday, March 11, he announced his awareness of an anonymous document and the call for a meeting, making clear his "disapprobation of such disorderly proceedings." Instead, he told the men, there would be another meeting five days later, on Saturday, March 15, to be presided over by "a proper representative of the staff of the Army"—someone, apparently, that Washington would designate for the task.[10]

This was, by design, a confusing message. On the one hand, Washington was expressing disapproval for what the conspirators were up to. On the other, it was unclear whether that disapproval was over their "disorderly" methods or the fact of their call for a meeting, which he affirmed would indeed be held. And yet Washington himself apparently wasn't going to be there because he was putting someone else in charge—perhaps so he could deny any involvement even as he managed the movement.

The conspirators were unwilling to surrender the initiative, however. The next day, March 12, a second Newburgh address appeared. Tuesday, Thursday, Saturday—whatever, it said. Washington, in his March 11 response, had "sanctified" their appeals. The important thing for soldiers to remember is that any meeting held under official auspices "cannot possibly lessen the *independence* of your sentiments."[11]

Washington, for his part, was also active that day. He reported to Elias Boudinot, the president of Congress, about what was happening. He reported as well to Congressman Jones, emphasizing that however wrongheaded the conspirators may be, the surest way to resolve the problem was for Congress to act responsibly. Washington also fired off a letter to Hamilton, whose letter of February 13 he now seemed to see in a new light. "There is something very mysterious in this business," Washington wrote. He never actually accused Hamilton of wrongdoing, but firmly asserted that a march on Philadelphia now would be a terrible idea, resulting in "a gulph of Civil horror from which there might be no receding."[12]

The ensuing days were quiet but tense. On the morning of the fifteenth, men gathered in the so-called New Building, which Washington had ordered built back in December to foster sociability among officers from different states. The presiding officer of the meeting was Horatio Gates—a man widely suspected then and since to have been involved in the conspiracy, though this has never been proven. As presiding officer, however, his job was to direct the proceedings without participating in debate. As Gates opened the meeting, Washington suddenly appeared. He asked for permission to speak, which Gates could hardly refuse.

Washington was in no mood to mince words. "Gentlemen: by an anonymous summons, an attempt has been made to convene you together," he began. "How inconsistent with the rules of propriety! How unmilitary!" He then moved on to the writer of the first address, admiring his cleverness, though "I could wish he had as much credit for the rectitude of his heart." Washington reminded the men he was deeply sympathetic to their grievances—and shared them. But he disapproved of what they were being told to do. He spoke of the anonymous author of the summons:

> If Peace takes place, never sheath your swords Says he until you have obtained full and ample justice; this dreadful alternative, of either deserting our Country in the extremest hour of her distress, or turning Arms against it, (which is the apparent object, unless Congress can be compelled into instant compliance) has something so shocking in it, that humanity revolts at the idea. My God! What can this writer have in view, by recommending such measures? Can he be a friend to the army? Can he be a friend to this Country? Rather, is he not an insidious foe?

Washington assured them he would do everything in his power to get them justice. But while he did so, "let me entreat you, Gentlemen, on your party, not to take any measures, which, viewed in the calm light of reason, will lessen the dignity, and sully the glory you have hitherto maintained."[13]

Accounts vary on the details of what happened next—Washington apparently had a letter from Congressman Jones he wished to read them—but all agreed that at some point in the process he fumbled for his reading glasses, something only those close to him had ever seen him wear. Washington, a man acutely conscious of his image, strived mightily to avoid anything that might compromise his sense of dignity or strength. But in the anxiety of the moment, he was apparently unconscious of merely personal considerations.

"Gentlemen," he reputedly said, "you'll permit me to put on my spectacles, for I have not only grown gray but almost blind in the service of my country."[14]

Whether because of the accumulated impact of Washington's remarks, or the unexpected display of vulnerability, the spectacles seemed to be the turning point. Grown men began to cry. Washington left the room. His trusted colleague, Knox, proposed motions that affirmed the army's "attachment to the rights and liberties of human nature" and its "unshaken confidence" in Congress.[15] They passed unanimously.

That's not to say everything ended happily ever after. Nationalists in Congress seized on the news emerging from the Newburgh Conspiracy to press their case in Congress, and got a deal on taxes and pensions—of a sort. But it was so riddled with compromises and half-measures that Hamilton himself would not endorse it. In the years that followed, many Revolutionary War veterans concluded they would never see the money they were owed and sold the promissory notes they had been issued, for pennies on the dollar, to speculators who bought them and then demanded they be paid at full value (something Hamilton successfully urged the government to do, to the disgust of his former ally, James Madison). Nor did Washington's Newburgh Address calm units elsewhere in the country. Detachments of drunken soldiers in Lancaster, Pennsylvania, actually marched on the capital in June 1783, surrounding fifteen members of Congress, Hamilton included, in the Pennsylvania Statehouse. The members were allowed to leave, and the uprising petered out, but the prestige of Congress was damaged.

These events may sound like something out of what we patronizingly call "a banana republic": sullen soldiers, rumors of intrigue, renegade detachments that are by turns threatening and incompetent. But with remarkable speed, a serious government crisis was all but forgotten. The Treaty of Paris was signed in September 1783, the Constitution was framed four years later, the pension issue was resolved, however unfairly, in the 1790s, and the wobbly filly of a nation grew strong and became a thoroughbred. The conspiracy that threatened the birth of our nation became little more than a footnote in American history.

Instead, Washington rode into the nation's capitol at Annapolis in December of 1783 and formally surrendered his military commission to civilian leaders. He did not style himself Caesar, the founder of an empire, but rather Cincinnatus, the Roman general who left the army and returned to his plow. In so doing, he made a pointed statement about the kind of nation he fought for, and how he hoped to be remembered. No less a figure than King George III predicted that if Washington acted on this intention, "he will be the greatest man in the world."[16]

Had Washington led, or failed to stop, the movement at Newburgh, could the United States have ended up like one of the rogue states that threaten world peace today? Maybe not. Perhaps Washington himself wasn't even a decisive factor. If he had styled himself a Napoleon or a Franco, much of the country might not have gone along with him. New England in particular was deeply suspicious of professional armies, which is why the crisis had emerged in the first place. Then again, this would hardly be the last time that a group of people brought about precisely what they were trying to avoid.

There is something we do know, however, and it's something that's not quite, or at least not entirely, a matter of luck: George Washington was a product of the circumstances of his birth, yes, but also a product of carefully considered values. Those values included a belief that people ruling themselves through what we've come to know as the democratic process was a very powerful one, and one he was willing to make considerable sacrifices for, including giving up home, family, and any income for eight years—and to place all these things at risk. He was willing to accept self-imposed limitations to honor those values and achieve the republic he believed would embody them, so much so that by the mid-1790s he was desperate to leave the presidency to which he had been twice unanimously elected so that he would not die in office, and so that power would be transferred smoothly and constitutionally. He was summoned back from his plow, but he finally did succeed in returning to it for good before his death in 1799.

In so doing, he honored his values, and realized his republican American Dream. Washington and his fellow Americans achieved something truly impressive: not simply winning their independence, but laying the foundations for centuries of representative government that included a head of state chosen in steady four-year intervals. They made it possible for the following stories to be told.

*(previous page)* MAN WITH A PLAN: Thomas Jefferson, engraved by Cornelius Tiebout after a portrait by Rembrandt Peale, circa 1801. The third president points to the Declaration of Independence, with the scientific contraptions of his fabled estate, Monticello, in the background. Jefferson was a man more comfortable with abstractions and scientific inquiry than the messy art of human relations—a reality nowhere more obvious than his duplicitous behavior with his predecessor, John Adams. (Presidential Portraits, Library of Congress)

CHAPTER ONE

# VICE PRESIDENT–ELECT JEFFERSON STABS A FRIEND IN THE BACK

*In which we see a hypocritical ideologue apprehend the value of pragmatism*

Sometime during the month of January 1797, Thomas Jefferson made a fateful decision that would betray a friendship and destabilize a nation. Elected Vice President of the United States the previous November, he secretly resolved to decline an invitation to collaborate closely in the new government of President John Adams. Instead, he would keep his distance and quietly aid the opposition. The Adams administration would in effect be doomed before it got underway. Even worse, Jefferson's decision would mean that the nation's first foreign policy crisis would spill over into domestic politics, rocking the country to its foundations.

The chief reason for Jefferson's decision to betray his friend was ideological. Adams, part of the so-called Federalist faction in the new political regime, favored a stronger central government and a foreign policy aligned with England. Jefferson, who belonged to the so-called Democratic-Republican faction, favored stronger state governments and a foreign policy aligned with France. Amid the tumult of the French Revolution, which careened between anarchy and authoritarianism, U.S.-French relations, so crucial to the success of the American Revolution, had deteriorated to the point where the two nations were at virtual war. President-elect Adams thought he could heal the breach, at home and abroad, by sending Jefferson—who had once been U.S. ambassador to France—to negotiate with the Revolutionary government. Even if Jefferson himself could not go, perhaps one of his allies, like Congressman James Madison, could. Adams would no doubt be excoriated by his Anglophile allies for such a move, but it was a risk he was willing to take—a bold act of solidarity in a fragile country that could ill afford internal squabbling.

Jefferson's first instinct was to accept the offer, discreetly extended through mutual friends.[1] Jefferson had known Adams for almost a quarter century; they had met in Philadelphia during the Second Continental Congress in 1775, collaborated on the Declaration of Independence the following year, and served together as diplomats in Europe during and after the American Revolution. In the years that followed they had drifted apart politically,[2] yet remained friendly amid increasingly obvious philosophical differences and their respective unhappiness with their roles in the Washington administration—Adams as vice president and Jefferson as secretary of state. (Jefferson, disgusted with Washington's bias toward Treasury Secretary Alexander Hamilton, left the nation's capitol in Philadelphia for his Virginia estate, Monticello, after the first term.) When Washington stepped down after his second term, Adams and Jefferson were widely considered the leading candidates from their respective factions to run for president. Adams won and became president, and as per the recently ratified Constitution, Jefferson, who came in second, became vice president.[3]

Not that Jefferson himself minded the outcome. In December 1796, Madison wrote Jefferson that since Adams was the likely winner, "you must prepare yourself therefore to be summoned to the place Mr. Adams now fills." Jefferson wrote back on New Year's Day of 1797 to say that was just fine with him: "I am his junior in life [Jefferson was nine years younger than

Adams], was his junior in Congress, his junior in the diplomatic line, his junior lately in our civil government." Besides, as he had noted in a December 27 letter to his South Carolinian friend Edward Rutledge, "this is certainly not the time to covet the helm." Given the difficulty any man would face in filling Washington's shoes, and the severity of the nation's foreign policy challenges, Jefferson was shrewd as well as gracious.[4]

The very next day, Jefferson went a step further, writing a warm letter to Adams himself, expressing satisfaction with the pending outcome. "No one then will congratulate you with purer disinterestedness than myself," he told his longtime collaborator. Indeed, he expressed relief. "The share indeed which I may have had in the late vote, I shall still value highly, as an evidence of the share I have in the esteem of my fellow citizens. . . . [But] I have no desire to govern men. It is a painful and thankless office." Jefferson went on to express the hope that Adams would be able to steer the nation away from a looming war with France. "If you are, the glory will be all your own; and that your administration may be filled with glory and happiness to yourself and advantage to us is the sincere wish of one who tho', in the course of our voyage thro' life, various little incidents have happened or been contrived to separate us, retains still for you the solid esteem of the moments when we were working for our independence, and sentiments of respect and affectionate attachment."[5]

Apparently, however, Jefferson had doubts about whether Adams should see the letter. We know this because rather than dispatching it directly, he sent it to his protégé, Congressman Madison, seeking his opinion. Madison was not ambivalent at all: He considered the letter a big mistake. He replied to Jefferson with a detailed list of reasons why Adams should never see it, the most important of which he saved for last: "Considering the probability that Mr. A's course of administration may force opposition to it from the Republican quarter, & the general uncertainty which our affairs may take, there may be real embarrassments from giving written possession to him."[6] Politics, Madison told Jefferson, comes before friendship.

Jefferson accepted this advice, reluctantly. "Mr. A. and myself were cordial friends from the beginning of the revolution," he explained in his reply of January 30. "The deviation from that line of policy on which we had been united has not made me less sensible of the rectitude of his heart: and I wished him to know this." Still, he would harden his heart and tow the party line: Adams may want his help, even invite his participation, but "both duty and inclination will shut that door to me." A month that began with Jefferson charting a course toward Adams ended with a resolution to head in the opposite direction.[7]

For his part, Adams—at times a vain and naïve man, though always an honest one—misunderstood the realities of American government in 1797, leading him to make some serious mistakes. His decision, for example, to emphasize continuity with the Washington administration by keeping on Washington's cabinet ignored the fact that many of these men were actually minions of Hamilton, who considered Adams an idiot (something Adams didn't fully understand, which probably only enhanced Hamilton's contempt). Adams was also slow to realize that Jefferson had cast his lot with the opposition, though this was clear to him by the time he officially took office.[8] Jefferson never announced his position—he hated personal confrontation and would rather dissemble than face acrimony—but his reserve was a statement in its own right. After attending a dinner with the departing Washington on March 6, 1797, the two men would not exchange a meaningful word for the next fifteen years.

Jefferson's shabby treatment of Adams was more than a personal failing: In a very real sense, it was a national tragedy. The American republic was never as fragile as it was during the Adams years, when the so-called Quasi War with France severely divided the nation, with both the Federalist and Democratic-Republican factions acting in deeply irresponsible ways. On one side, supporters of the war rounded up and imprisoned those who expressed dissent as part of the Alien and Sedition Acts—a set of bills Adams signed against his better instincts and that permanently marred his reputation. On the other, critics of the administration, among them majorities in the Virginia and Kentucky legislatures, with help from Madison and Jefferson respectively, drew up resolutions that states could simply ignore federal laws they did not like, raising the dangerous specter of secession. Amid wartime preparations Adams hoped would be headed by former president Washington, who instead delegated the task to the power-hungry Hamilton—a truly frightening prospect—the president ultimately steered the nation on a path to peace by ignoring earlier snubs by the French government and trying again with a more receptive set of French diplomats. But the job might have been a lot easier, and the partisan divisions that rocked the nation to its foundations would have been a lot less severe, had Jefferson helped Adams navigate the shoals.

But that was the thing about Jefferson: He had a restless mind that could stray remarkably, even alarmingly, far from pragmatic considerations. No less a figure than Madison observed in 1832 that "allowances ought to be made for a habit in Mr. Jefferson as in others of great genius of expressing in strong and round terms, impressions of the moment."[9] (Of course, in this particular case, Jefferson had been following Madisonian counsel.) The most obvious example of Jefferson's tendency to round square truths, now invoked endlessly, is the fact that the man who wrote "all men are created equal" was, to his dying day, a slaveholder. At least those five words had a stirring idealism about them. Other notions were a good deal more strange, even repellent, like his desire to reduce happiness to a mathematical equation, or his suggestion, after much calculation of average life spans, that no contracts should be binding after twenty years. The complexities of lived experience were elusive, if not repugnant, to him. Even Jefferson's attempt to rewrite the New Testament by making the words of Jesus a set of ethical precepts has an aridity that suggests that his celebrated invocations of religious tolerance were little more than evidence of his detachment, even indifference, toward the complexities of spiritual life.

When he had his own turn in the presidency, Jefferson hewed as closely as he could to his theory of limited government. But, he would realize with some regret, this could be difficult. Nowhere was this more obvious than in dealing with the prospect of the greatest real estate transaction of all time. Here, as elsewhere, immediate opportunity clashed with abstract philosophy. It is a measure of the depth of Jefferson's commitments that it was unclear to him which he should choose.

Jefferson's accession to the presidency came in the notorious election of 1800, an election in which he challenged, and defeated, an Adams hobbled by the Alien and Sedition Acts and divisions among the Federalists. But Jefferson almost lost what he sought because of the deal he cut with Aaron Burr. The bargain was that Burr would deliver New York's electoral votes to Jefferson, and Jefferson would deliver the vice-presidency to Burr. However, this arrangement took an unexpected turn when he and Burr finished tied in the Electoral College, precipitating a fierce intrafactional struggle. Ironically, the conniving Alexander Hamilton, who detested both men, held the balance of power and directed his supporters to back a Jefferson he detested less. (Burr would kill Hamilton in a duel over an obscure slander three years later.)

The election of 1800 was a major turning point in American history. Though not immediately obvious at the time, it marked the beginning of the end of the Federalists, whose avowedly elitist approach to politics was ill-suited to a country where barriers to voting were falling and electoral participation was rising. Jefferson established a changed tone by the relative modesty with which he was inaugurated, projecting an image of republican simplicity—one, it should be said, markedly at odds with the facts of his life—that contributed to his mythic stature as the champion of democracy. At the same time, he lived up to his reputation for graciousness in his famed inaugural address, in which the magnanimous victor proclaimed "that we are all republicans, we are all federalists. . . . Every difference of opinion is not a difference of principle."[10]

Jefferson's first term in office was a smashing success. He pursued and realized Republican goals of cutting taxes, balancing the federal budget, slimming down the military, and (especially) undoing the ravages of the Alien and Sedition Acts by dropping cases and letting the laws lapse. To a great extent, he was lucky—his accession to the presidency coincided with a lull in the raging conflict between Britain and France, which meant that the

United States was, for the moment at least, not storm-tossed between them. This allowed him to concentrate on domestic policy. It also presented him with a fabulous opportunity.

When Jefferson ascended to the presidency in 1801, the western boundary of the United States was the Mississippi River. The Mississippi and its tributaries, especially the Ohio, were increasingly viewed as indispensable avenues of national growth. The main thrust of American settlement was west of the Allegheny Mountains into the new states of Ohio, Kentucky, and Tennessee. But expansionists, ranging from landless farmers to the president himself, looked to the southwest in particular with growing interest. American leaders hoped to persuade Spain, which controlled most of the continent, thanks to the French cession of Louisiana, to part not only with New Orleans, but the Floridas (whose east and west sections formed the northern rim of the Caribbean, which Spain had long held as a buffer zone for its valuable, and far more highly prized, holdings in Central America, South America, and the islands off the Gulf of Mexico).

What Jefferson didn't anticipate was the return of a former player on the scene: France. By the start of his administration, that revolution-wracked nation had come full circle and was now governed by Napoleon Bonaparte, an autocrat in all but name (he would be crowned Emperor in 1804). The very interval of peace between France and Britain that had allowed Jefferson to focus on domestic policy also gave Napoleon the opportunity to survey the global situation, and this led him to conclude that France should reestablish the North American empire it lost to England in the Seven Years War of 1754–63 (a war that, in driving France from the continent, made it safe for British colonies to revolt against the mother country). The point of reentry, Napoleon resolved, would be Santo Domingo, a French possession on the island of Hispaniola (today known as the nation of Haiti, which shares the island with the Dominican Republic).

This was a decision replete with ironies. For one thing, it forced Jefferson to wrestle with his feelings about France, where he had lived as U.S. ambassador from 1784 to 1789. For almost three decades, he looked to that nation as a source of hope and help for his own nation. "A more benevolent people, I have never known," he wrote at the end of his life, "nor greater warmth & devotedness in their select friendships. Their kindness and accommodation to strangers is unparalleled, and the hospitality of Paris is beyond anything I had conceived to be practicable in a large city."[11] Jefferson considered France the preeminent nation on the face of the earth, and had trouble accepting the fact that it was now a competitor on the North American continent.

The complications didn't stop there. Jefferson considered French revolutionary ideals to be a beacon to the world, maintaining such beliefs in the face of growing skepticism on the part of his own countrymen—and geopolitical situations that exposed the selfishness and contradictions inherent in both French and American notions of freedom. In 1791, explicitly invoking the French Revolutionary ideals of liberty and equality, a slave revolt eventually headed by the former domestic servant Toussaint L'Ouverture succeeded in overthrowing colonial rule in Haiti. A French general persuaded him to accept rule by the revolutionary republic, but Toussaint never surrendered his authority to Paris, effectively governing the country. The Adams administration, believing the 1778 American treaty with France non-transferable after the fall of Louis XVI, actively aided Touissant, much to the chagrin of Southerners like Jefferson, who were appalled by the precedent a successful slave revolt might portend for the United States.

So when the Napoleonic government asked the new Jefferson administration for its help in subjugating the would-be colony, Jefferson eagerly agreed, unaware that he would be serving larger French colonial ambitions. "Nothing would be easier than to supply everything for your army and navy, and to starve out Toussaint," he told the secretary to the French delegation in Washington.[12] Yet even as the American and French governments were having these discussions—even as the Treaty of Mortefontaine, which officially ended the Quasi War between the United States and France, was going through its final procedural steps before its final ratification in 1801—Napoleon was following through on the provisions of the Treaty of San Ildefonso (1800), a secret Franco-Spanish pact by which the Louisiana territory would be returned to France. Unwittingly, then, Jefferson would be helping Napoleon use Santo Domingo as a springboard to occupy the very territory on which he was pinning his own hopes. It was precisely the kind of Machiavellian move that the French foreign minister, Charles Maurice de Talleyrand, loved to execute, particularly when it came to Americans.[13] For Talleyrand, Louisiana was to become a "wall of brass"[14] that would stop American western expansion cold.

As was so often the case, it was Madison, now serving as secretary of state, who reconnected Jeffersonian dreams with factual realities. Madison learned from the U.S. ambassador to England, Rufus King, of the rumored French takeover of Louisiana, and brought it to Jefferson's attention. The two agreed to send an envoy, Robert Livingston of New York, to find out what was going on. Livingston arrived in Paris at the end of 1801 and spent the next year enduring Napoleonic evasion and the thinly veiled insults of Talleyrand as he pumped his sources for information on who controlled what, and if, when, or whether territory was actually going to change hands.

Meanwhile, Napoleon dispatched an army to overthrow Touissant in early 1802. This part of his global design ran into unexpected difficulties, not only because of the resistance French forces encountered from the former slaves, but also because of the mosquito-borne Yellow Fever that decimated the French forces sent to the island. Madison demonstrated that two could play a game of diplomatic duplicity by unexpectedly failing to deliver the promised support for the invasion. The situation on Santo Domingo became so serious that Napoleon assembled an entirely new force to send there, one that was ordered to move on to Louisiana immediately upon the subjugation of the island. Yet a combination of bad weather and wary British surveillance (the fleet was held back in part to avoid suspicions of its use as a possible invasion force) hampered the departure of the armada, which remained marooned off the coast of Holland in 1802–03.

There were other complications as well. By early 1803 Spain had still not formally relinquished control of Louisiana, in part because of ongoing dickering over the terms of the Treaty of San Ildefonso. Spain had also—for reasons that remain unclear, and in apparent violation of a 1795 treaty—revoked U.S. access to

New Orleans. This move triggered a firestorm of angry reaction in American public opinion. Federalists in particular pushed for a hard line in response to the move, demanding that the Jefferson administration prepare for war. Jefferson, for his part, was deeply worried as well, but sought to avoid a military solution, in part because the newly slimmed-down armed forces were not in much of a position to provide one. He nevertheless mobilized military forces under the direction of General James Wilkinson (unaware that Wilkinson was in the pay of the Spanish foreign ministry), even as he enlisted his longtime ally James Monroe to go to Paris, authorized to buy New Orleans and/or Florida.

Napoleon, for his part, was having second thoughts about the whole North American adventure. The tense 1802 Anglo-French Treaty of Amiens was breaking down amid mutual distrust, and he was beginning to think he'd be better off having a showdown with England: Maybe that fleet off the coast of Holland could be used for an invasion of Britain after all. Though it was far from clear he had the legal right to do so, he decided to sell the whole Spanish package—the port of New Orleans, the Louisiana territory, whatever part of the Floridas were his to trade—to the Americans. He'd use the money in the fight against England and then, exploiting any number of possible ambiguities, circle back and reclaim the territory later. Monroe arrived in Paris in the spring of 1803 just as an incredulous Livingston was learning of the proposed sale, desperately seeking to get the credit for a transaction bigger than either envoy was technically authorized to make, but an offer that was simply too good to refuse. The British, regarding American ownership of Louisiana as the lesser of two evils, agreed to loan the Americans the money (U.S. credit was excellent, thanks to Alexander Hamilton, whose financial instincts were as sound as his personal scruples suspicious). The transaction, which would cost about $15 million—$23.5 million after interest and including claims from the Quasi War—would come to about 4¢ for each 838,000 acres, more than doubling the size of the nation.[15]

At this point, another source of trouble became apparent: Thomas Jefferson himself. Though the president had given his blessing to pursue the purchase of Louisiana, he got cold feet when confronted with the necessity of exercising executive authority in a speedy and direct manner. The ultimate exponent of limited government, the man who viewed the very executive power he wielded with suspicion, Jefferson did not believe he had sufficient authority to consummate the deal. The only way to do it, he told his cabinet, was through a constitutional amendment. Madison, now secretary of state, was among those who tried to talk him out of proposing one: The president had the constitutional treaty-making power, Madison (the principal author of that document) told him. All through the summer of 1803, Jefferson remained adamant. He even wrote drafts of the amendment himself. The problem, as even he realized, however, was that the terms of the deal required the United States to sign by the end of October, and Congress wasn't even supposed to meet again until November.

Foreign leaders forced Jefferson's hand. He received word from Livingston that Napoleon was railing against the agreement, demanding it be rendered void if payment was late. King Carlos IV of Spain, for his part, was complaining that Napoleon had broken his promise not to transfer the property once he received it. According to Livingston, Spain and France needed no more than the "slightest pretence" to scotch the deal. It's now or never, he told Jefferson.

Jefferson called for a special session of Congress to meet in October. The Republican majority leader in the Senate, Wilson Cary Nicholas of Virginia, begged the president not even to mention the word "amendment," fearing Federalists and more conservative Republicans would refuse to adopt the treaty-based approach to the deal.

This was the moment of truth: Would Jefferson honor his notions of the way he thought the world should work, or act on the realities of the moment? Reluctantly, a president who had hoped to "set an example against broad construction"[16] went along with the plan. Despite Federalist hostility to the acquisition (Alexander Hamilton, who favored national aggrandizement in any form, was a notable exception), the proposal cleared both houses of Congress. On December 20, 1803—three weeks after Spain had formally handed over the territory—the French flag was lowered and the Stars and Stripes were raised on the river-side Place d'Armes in New Orleans. Louisiana became American territory. And Jefferson became a pragmatist.

Lots of loose ends remained. One was the question of Florida—how much, if any, the United States was entitled to under the deal, a question Napoleon had refused to engage during the negotiations. (It would be another fifteen years until this matter was resolved by General Andrew Jackson, who in effect presented Spain with an ultimatum: Sell it or lose it.) Other issues were shrouded in mystery, then and ever since. Jefferson still had no idea that his chief military officer, General James Wilkinson, was in the pay of the Spanish government. Moreover, Wilkinson, serving as governor of the Louisiana territory, was actively collaborating with the fugitive Aaron Burr, who, following his murder of Hamilton and ejection from the vice presidency after Jefferson's reelection in 1804, moved to Ohio and began to raise a private army with Wilkinson as part of a murky plot to create a new southwestern conspiracy. (Here was Jefferson's decentralized dream as nightmare: a confederacy of competing and autonomous states.) Wilkinson got cold feet and betrayed Burr, who was arrested and brought back to Washington to be tried for treason. Jefferson was desperate to see Burr hang, but was thwarted by another hated antagonist, the arch-Federalist Chief Justice of the Supreme Court, John Marshall, who presided over the trial and demanded that any testimony against Burr be corroborated by at least two independent witnesses (in the process, setting a legal standard for evaluating hearsay). Burr was acquitted and lived until 1836. But he proved to be the last major threat to untrammeled American occupation of Louisiana—and beyond.

Such subplots notwithstanding, the Louisiana Purchase has always been viewed as a triumph for Jefferson, the capstone for one of the most successful presidential administrations in American history. Even before the deal was complete, Jefferson had secretly arranged an expedition—supposedly for scientific purposes, but in fact for more strategic ones—to be led by Meriwether Lewis and William Clark. Their legendary journey in 1804–05 mapped the territory, laid the foundations for trade, and raised awareness of the importance of the west for American development. Jefferson cruised to reelection in 1804 (dumping Burr for New York governor George Clinton), defeating South Carolinian Charles Pinckney with a crushing 162 electoral votes to 14, further hastening the decline of the Federalists.

Alas, in the years that followed Jefferson returned to ideological form. By all accounts, his second term was as bad as his first was good, establishing the conventional wisdom for second presidential terms that remains with us to this day. A large part of the reason for this, as it had been for Washington and Adams, was the raging conflict between Britain and France. Warfare between them officially resumed at the end of 1803—the remaining French forces on Santo Domingo surrendered to a British fleet cruising offshore in November—and got going in earnest again in 1805 (though Napoleon never did manage to launch that British invasion). No American administration could have completely escaped being caught in the middle. But Jefferson's highly idealized policy of agrarian self-sufficiency compounded the problem when he imposed an embargo on trade with both powers, a move that hurt American trade far more than anything Britain or France did. It even led to talk among some New Englanders for secession—an option that was to float around American politics for about four score and seven years after the nation's founding.

When one considers how committed Jefferson remained to a vision of limited government—a vision to which his attachment would only grow in the remaining years of his life—the really striking thing is not the self-evident logic of the Louisiana Purchase but his willingness to suspend his instinctive aversion to centralized power necessary to realize it. The explanation for this anomaly, as historian Joseph Ellis has indicated, is the "special, indeed almost mystical, place the West had in his thinking. When history presented him with an unexpected and unprecedented opportunity to eliminate forever the presence on America's western border of any major European power (Spain did not count here), it triggered his most visionary energies, which then overrode his traditional republican injunctions. For Jefferson more than any other figure in the revolutionary generation, the West was America's future."[17]

At a few key moments in his life, Jefferson was able to put aside abstractions and respond concretely to the demands of the moment. The Louisiana Purchase was one such instance. Five years earlier, he had failed a crucial test of character with Adams, where statesmanship and decency had both demanded forthright solidarity. Fortunately, that failure did not prove fatal, either for the country or the friendship. After Jefferson left office, the two mortals resumed an epistolary friendship that continued to their shared dying day of July 4, 1826. Some things, they both knew, were more important than diplomacy, or philosophy, or politics.

*(previous page)* DOING IT BY THE BOOK: John Quincy Adams, by Asher Brown Durand, 1826. A formal intellectual never comfortable with the hurly burly of American politics, Adams tried and failed to remain above the fray while president—but discovered his inner firebrand after his opponents succeeded in driving him out of office. (Presidential Portraits, Library of Congress)

CHAPTER TWO

# FORMER PRESIDENT ADAMS CAN'T STOP GAGGING

*In which we see that a privileged
upbringing need not handicap a (very)
senior citizen*

It was an inauguration of legendary proportions. An estimated 20,000 well-wishers, most of them uninvited and many of them wearing coonskin caps, broke a cable intended to cordon off the official party, turning the White House into a frat house. The liquor flowed freely in large tubs, which is no doubt why so much of the furniture was trashed (and why some partygoers reputedly fell out of windows). The crowd was so boisterous that the new president would be forced to spend his first night in office at a local hotel—and General Andrew Jackson, not a man who typically made even tactical retreats, made this one on horseback.

This eleventh inauguration, held on March 4, 1829, stands out not only for its intensity, but also for its symbolic significance. Jackson was the first man from a western state (Tennessee) to become president, and his election was widely regarded as a triumph of democracy. For some, this celebration was a matter of vindication; Jackson had won the popular vote four years earlier, but was denied the presidency due to the vicissitudes of the Electoral College, which had been designed precisely as a circuit breaker of surges in popular passion. But such surges could not be contained forever, and it was now clear that the energies represented by the ascendant Jackson were no passing fad but rather the beginnings of a new political order.

Amid the dignitaries and the democratic throng who gathered to usher in this new order, one figure was conspicuously absent from the official ceremonies: former president John Quincy Adams. While he could hardly be expected to celebrate the occasion (especially this former president, who was not the kind of man who enjoyed merrymaking), it was an established custom that the departing and arriving chief executives would participate in the public transition of power. This was a ritual freighted with symbolic significance. That the outgoing leader would decline to attend—that he would slip out of the capital quietly the night before, desperate to avoid the inauguration—was a violation of protocol, even an insult to democracy. Many of those who actually noticed his absence no doubt chalked it up to the very characteristics that had cost Adams his job in the first place: humorlessness, hauteur, and a failure to recognize, much less accept, the emergence of a new common sense. It was sad, really, for this pathetic shadow of a man to be so out of touch.

John Quincy Adams was not the first president, however, to skip his successor's inauguration. Twenty-eight years earlier, his father, John Adams, who couldn't bear the thought of participating in the triumph of the two-faced Thomas Jefferson, had also left town the night before. Up until this point, the two Adamses were the only American presidents who had failed to win reelection, both defeated by men—Jefferson and Jackson—who represented the affirmation of an emerging democratic tradition. (To this day, they are symbolically linked in the annual Jefferson-Jackson Day dinner that is a fixture of the Washington social scene.) John Adams had left the White House in 1801 and lived another 25 years in relative obscurity. Now his son seemed headed for a similar fate.

It wasn't supposed to end like this. The oldest son of formidable parents, John Quincy Adams—or "JQA," as he was known—literally had a front-row seat for some of the defining moments in American history. He was seven years old when his mother Abigail took him to Bunker Hill in June 1775 to witness a pivotal early battle in the American Revolution (dad was in Philadelphia as a member of the Continental Congress). He was ten when his father took him along to Paris as part of an American delegation seeking aid from France. His French was so good that JQA was appointed, at the age of 14, to be the interpreter for the U.S. minister to Russia, a mission he took unaccompanied by his father. He toured the continent before returning, in 1783, to the senior Adams, who promptly made the 16-year-old his private secretary. Ironically, this child's provincial parents feared their cosmopolitan boy wasn't provincial enough, and so sent him back home to relatively rustic Harvard College, which he entered as a junior. Upon his graduation in 1787, he went on to study law, a subject he didn't have much feeling for but one that might prove useful.

Over the course of the next 35 years, Adams lived an exceptionally busy life that included marriage, four children, stints in the Massachusetts legislature and the U.S. Senate, a professorship at Harvard, and appointment to the U.S. Supreme Court—an honor he declined. He did so in large measure because the real focus in his life in these years was diplomacy. At one point or another Adams not only represented the United States at The Hague, but also in Berlin, London, and St. Petersburg, where he became a walking companion of the tsar of Russia. He saw the rise and fall of Napoleon Bonaparte firsthand, as French armies invaded countries where he was posted. And he participated in negotiating treaties with Napoleon's rival, Great Britain, in agreements that stretched from Jay's Treaty in 1795 to the Treaty of Ghent, which ended the War of 1812 two years later. From there he went on to become secretary of state for eight years in the Monroe administration (1817–1825). Adams conceived and wrote the Monroe Doctrine, whereby the United States would view European intervention in the Western Hemisphere as an unfriendly act (a policy that Britain, with the naval muscle to support it, was happy to endorse for its own reasons). He was also a pivotal figure behind the Adams-Onis Treaty, which made Florida part of the United States. To a great degree, this happened because Adams strongly supported the highly controversial actions of General Jackson, who chased hostile Seminole Indians into Spanish Florida, convincing the Spanish government that it should sell the territory for cash before losing it in battle.

The presidency thus seemed like the logical culmination of such a long and distinguished career. There were, however, two big obstacles in the way. The first was Adams himself. No one ever denied the man was smart; but in politics, as in much else, being smart isn't enough. Adams lacked the warmth and flexibility that were the hallmarks of the best politicians. "The tendency to dissipation at Paris seems to be irresistible," he wrote in his diary in 1815, a somewhat typical sentiment from a child of the Puritans.[1] His fellow negotiators working on the Treaty of Ghent stayed up playing cards until 4:00 AM—the hour in which he typically got up. Adams was the kind of guy you would be very happy to have at the negotiating table, but unless you liked to read the Bible in Hebrew, perhaps not the kind of guy you would be comfortable with at the dinner table. He irritated his partners during the peace talks by eating alone because he didn't like the cigars they smoked and the bad wine they drank.

The other big obstacle Adams faced was not internal, but environmental. At the very moment his attainment of the presidential prize might have seemed like a foregone conclusion, the American political system was also undergoing one of the most decisive transformations in its history. And Adams, to put it simply, was yesterday's man. Ever since his father had lost his job, the presidency had been passed down with little electoral contentiousness. (Jefferson's election in 1800 had been an exception.) Now, though, a number of people were contending for the position, people who were not inclined to defer to JQA's obvious qualifications, among them General Jackson. Adams's dilemma—wanting the job but not wanting to want it; wishing to avoid campaigning when only campaigning would make victory possible—is evocatively suggested by a diary entry in the spring of 1824:

When I consider that to me alone, of all the candidates before the nation, failure of success would be equivalent to a vote of censure by the nation upon my past service, I cannot dissemble that I have more at stake upon the result than any other individual in the Union. Yet a man qualified for the elective Chief Magistracy of ten millions of people should be a man proof alike to prosperous and adverse fortune. If I am able to bear success, I must be tempered to endure defeat.[2]

The presidential election of 1824 was one of the more convoluted ones in American history. Jackson won both the electoral and popular vote, but he failed to get a majority of either, throwing the election into the House of Representatives, where each state would get one vote. After a protracted struggle, Adams emerged as the winner in February 1825, largely because another rival, Henry Clay, threw his support to him. When Adams then appointed Clay as secretary of state—there's a legendary silence in the otherwise exhaustive JQA diary about whether the two cut a deal—charges of a "corrupt bargain" began that dogged Adams for the next four years. If indeed he could have known what the future would bring, he might well have chosen not to bear success after all.

The "corrupt bargain" was only part of the problem. While Adams tried to maintain the old above-the-fray ideals of the Founding Fathers, a newly mobilized group of small-government Jeffersonians, now simply calling themselves "Democrats," dedicated themselves to making Adams miserable. Policies he supported, like strong cooperation with the new nations of Latin America, were widely scoffed at, particularly by white North Americans who deemed South and Central Americans as their inferiors. Relative moderation in dealings with Native American peoples was also fiercely resisted. Adams's proposal for federal government support for a national university was mocked, and his idea for the founding of an astronomical laboratory, his call for "lighthouses *of* the sky" was lampooned as "lighthouses *in* the sky."[3] However far-seeing such ideas might seem in retrospect, Adams was hopelessly out of touch with his times, and lacked the give-and-take social skills that might have made his ideas more palatable. The Democrats, fully mobilized and in righteous fury over their "defeat" in 1824, secured an unmistakable victory for Jackson in 1828. It was a new day in American politics.

And the sun was clearly setting for 61-year-old John Quincy Adams—or, more accurately, a particular version of John Quincy Adams, the diplomatic statesman who strived to live and work above the fray. But the Puritan work ethic still burned brightly in the old man, who was not quite ready to go into serene retirement. A group of old Federalist friends worked to procure him a congressional seat in his hometown of Quincy, Massachusetts, which he was able to win in 1830 without campaigning and by a large margin. For the first and only time, a former chief executive took a seat in the House of Representatives. And as that first term became a second and a third—he would be elected nine times, serving from 1831 to 1848—a new John Quincy Adams came to life.

There were any number of issues that engendered significant debate in the years Adams served in Congress: whether or not there should be a Bank of the United States (Jackson ultimately destroyed the bank in one of the signal acts of his career); whether or not "civilized" Indian tribes in the southeast had a legal right to their lands (Jackson forcibly expelled them); whether or not South Carolina could "nullify" a federal law, specifically an onerous tariff, that its government considered oppressive ("over my dead body," Jackson replied, and the South Carolinians backed down—this time, anyway). Adams opposed Jackson when it came to economic and Indian policy, and strongly supported him in the Nullification crisis. During the 1830s an opposition to Jacksonian Democrats coalesced in the form of a new political party, the Whigs, and while Adams generally took Whig positions on the issues of the day, he remained an independent-minded maverick never particularly close with party insiders.

By this point, it was well understood by all involved that, like it or not, American politics was a matter of partisanship (the Adams-Clay deal was mild by comparison) and debate. But with all these economic and governmental debates raging, there was one issue that Congress wasn't at all eager to take up in those years: slavery. This was a topic virtually no one in power wanted to talk about—and hadn't wanted to talk about for decades. The Constitution never mentions the word at all, tap-dancing around it with phrases like "three-fifths of all other persons" in the so-called three-fifths compromise or "person held to Service or Labour" in the fugitive slave clause, which required escaped slaves to be returned to their owners. The issue was broached a handful of times: James Madison skillfully channeled a Quaker abolitionist petition into parliamentary oblivion in 1790; and the Missouri Compromise of 1819–20 contained what had been some explosive disagreement. But the rancor of that debate convinced many politicians that like the subject of religion at Thanksgiving dinner, the less said the better.

The problem was that events outside Washington were making the subject harder to avoid. In August 1831, four months before Adams took his seat in the House, the notorious slave insurrection of Nat Turner struck terror into the heart of the South. Turner's rebellion was put down swiftly. Yet the potential for mayhem was always there, and in response, the Virginia legislature actually considered abolishing slavery in 1832. The idea was debated, rejected, and then swept under the rug.

In the short term, however, abolitionists posed little threat to slave owners (nor, for that matter, to the New England companies that financed and insured them), because virtually all Americans regarded abolitionists as a lunatic fringe. Moreover, slave interests were deeply entrenched in the U.S. government: With the exception of the Adamses, every president through Jackson had been a slaveholder, and even subsequent ones who weren't (like Jackson's handpicked successor, Martin Van Buren) cooperated with them. The Chief Justice of the Supreme Court from the mid-1830s to the mid-1860s was slaveholding Roger Taney. The admission of new slave states from Kentucky (1792) through Texas (1845) guaranteed that slaveholders would exert significant, if not decisive, power.

And during Adams's Congressional career, proslavery advocates were flexing their muscles. By the mid-1830s, this faction and its sympathizers decided the best way to preserve their power was simply to shut down discussion. It had long been a tradition to devote the opening of every congressional session, and some segment of time during the months that followed, to receiving petitions from ordinary citizens. By this point, however, more and more of these petitions concerned slavery. For a long time, such petitions were ceremoniously ignored through a standard procedure of tabling them or referring them to a committee that would end up producing the legislative equivalent of a form letter. Now slavery's defenders sought to shut down debate in a more formal way. Southern congressmen proposed to do so by enacting a "gag rule" that would automatically table slavery petitions and remove the subject from discussion entirely.

This proved to be a turning point for Adams. Like many of his contemporaries, he had little appetite before the 1830s for speaking out about slavery, and tended to look skeptically on the new abolitionist movement, whose aims and methods he regarded as impractical, if not downright counterproductive. This isn't to say he lacked convictions on the issue. After all, he was an Adams. His father had always been opposed to slavery; his mother perhaps even more so. As a United States senator, JQA complained about the three-fifths compromise, advocated for hearing a Quaker petition for restraining the spread of slavery, and unsuccessfully promoted a tax on imported slaves. During the Missouri furor of 1820, Adams privately described slavery as "the great and foul stain upon the North American Union, and it is a contemplation worthy of the most exalted soul whether its total abolition is or isn't practicable." He speculated that "a dissolution, at least temporary, of the Union, as now constituted, would be certainly necessary. . . . The Union might then be reorganized on the fundamental principle of emancipation. This object is vast in its compass, awful in its prospects, sublime and beautiful in its issue."[4] But JQA kept such views to himself; after all, for most of his career he had been a professional diplomat.

Now, however, Adams began to see slavery as an issue that intersected with many others—and one he felt morally obligated to speak out on. One could view JQA's behavior in ensuing years as a late, feisty counterattack on the people who made him miserable while president. You could also see the fight he went on to lead as a passionate struggle for civil rights, specifically free speech. Yet it's finally impossible to separate either of these imperatives from the way slavery was entwining so many aspects of national life like a toxic weed. Even before the gag rule became a formal proposal, Adams identified what was at stake in refusing to even hear what ordinary citizens had to say in their petitions, even those opinions he disliked himself. "You suppress the right of petition; you suppress freedom of the press; you suppress freedom of religion," he told proponents of the gag rule in December 1835. The best way to prevent a protracted debate, he said, was to let these people have their say, and then "we will hear no more about this exciting subject."[5] Such advice was ignored; the gag rule passed the House in early 1836.

Actually the gag rule was only one item in a broader set of proslavery proposals to be voted on that spring. The first, and presumably least objectionable, was affirmation of a common-sense statement: "Congress possesses no constitutional authority to interfere in any way with the institution of slavery in any of the states." Whether or not slavery could spread to the territories was an increasingly important question, but what already admitted states did about "the peculiar institution" was presumably their own business. Yet when it came time for Adams to verbally record his vote, he asked whether he could have five minutes to explain why this resolution was "false and utterly untrue." Proslavery House members who weren't shocked—even most *antislavery* members took slavery in the South for granted—shouted to call Adams to order. Tired of wrangling, and wary of getting ensnared in an argument that could get out of control, the House dropped the subject to consider other business.

The subject shifted to a resolution to provide relief to refugees in Alabama and Georgia, who had been displaced in American conflicts with Seminole Indians. Adams got the floor again, and taking advantage of a parliamentary technicality that would allow him to connect this topic to a previous one, launched into an explanation of a scenario whereby Congress could, completely constitutionally, interfere in slavery where it already existed: in wartime. "From the instant that your slaveholding states become the theatre of war, civil, servile, or foreign, from that instant the war powers of Congress extend to interference with the institution of slavery in every way by which it can be interfered with," he explained. An astonished Pennsylvanian asked Adams if he had heard him correctly: Was JQA saying that in the event of a slave insurrection, for example, the Constitution would end? No, Adams replied; the *Constitution* wouldn't end, but *slavery* might.

> The very fact of the people of a free portion of the Union marching to the support of the masters would [itself] be an interference with those institutions; and that, in the event of a war, the result of which no man could tell, the treaty-making power [something the federal government very explicitly reserves to itself and not the states] would come to be equivalent to universal emancipation [in such a scenario].[6]

In 1836, however, most members of the House considered JQA's reasoning absurdly theoretical, and the resolution affirming the rights of the states to control slavery, like the one regarding the Seminoles and gag rule itself, passed by crushing margins. Adams's assertion that the gag order was a direct violation of the Constitution was shouted down by other members, and for the rest of the congressional session, the subject of slavery was forbidden.

But what about the next session? As soon as it convened in 1837, Adams introduced a petition praying for the end of the slave trade in Washington. Can he even do that, his opponents asked? Yes, replied Speaker James Polk—the gag expired with the last Congress. So they tabled the petition. A series of maneuvers followed, culminating in a new gag rule, which passed by a 2–1 margin.

Well, asked Adams, what about the petitions that were brought up *before* this new gag took effect? Could *they* be discussed? After more wrangling, the answer was no. Hmmm, he replied; I have here some petitions that sort of fall into a gray area. Take this one, from nine ladies of Fredericksburg, Virginia—Adams didn't want to name them for their own safety—praying for the end of the slave trade in Washington. He wasn't even sure if it was legitimate. Didn't matter: The petition was immediately tabled. But there was bait at the end of this line. Later in the day, JQA's colleague, John Patton of Virginia, who had grown up in Fredericksburg, had a look at the petition. There are no ladies (i.e., gentlewomen) who signed this petition, he said on the House floor, and if the gentleman from Massachusetts had only asked him, he could have made that clear. Patton only recognized one of the names, and that was from a free mulatto woman, and she was "of infamous character."

Oh really? "How does the gentleman know it?" Adams asked. "I did not say I knew the woman personally," Patton responded. Well, that's good, said Adams.

> I am glad the gentleman now says he does not know these women, for if he did not disclaim that knowledge, I might have asked who it was that made these women infamous—whether it was those of their own color or their masters. I have understood that there are those among the coloured portion of the slave-holding states, who bear the image of their masters.

According to the transcript from the *Congressional Globe*, a "great sensation" followed this rapier-sharp sexual allusion.[7]

Adams wasn't done tweaking his adversaries that day. He had another petition. This one was also complicated, because it happened to come from slaves, some of whom could not write and only made their mark. He would submit to the rules of the House as they pertain to petitions from U.S. citizens, but how do the rules of the House apply to petitions that come from those who aren't full citizens?

Speaker Polk described himself as "baffled." One member suggested that Southern congressmen should walk out in protest. Another suggested the slave petition be set on fire right there on the House floor. Multiple members cried out: "Expel him!" Cooler heads prevailed: a resolution was drafted merely censuring Adams for "extending to slaves a privilege only belonging to freemen, directly incit[ing] the slave population to insurrection."

There's only one problem, Adams observed when things quieted down enough for him to reply. His adversaries apparently had not read the petition: No one was talking about an insurrection. These slaves were asking that slavery be *preserved* in the District of

Columbia. (In fact, this petition was probably a hoax, which Adams then turned to his advantage.) When one of his colleagues replied that he would just as soon hear a petition from a horse or dog, Adams assured the congressman that if a horse or dog ever did send him a petition, he would be sure to try and introduce it. Southerners were not amused, and no resolution of the matter was reached.

Even those who ostensibly supported Adams paid him only the most backhanded of compliments. "It would be unjust to believe that, in the prime and vigor of manhood, the honorable member would have adopted the course of action which, at this late stage of his life, seems to control him," said Representative Abijah Mann of New York. "The high noontide of his life has long since passed with him, and its wane is no doubt upon him, before he is either aware or sensible of it." The less than senile Adams, sitting right there, no doubt wondered whether friends like these made enemies unnecessary.[8]

But he didn't care. Every year, from 1836 to 1840, he tried to introduce petitions to end slavery, and every year the gag rule was invoked or renewed. Nor did the invective or threats stop him from making proposals like one in 1838 sarcastically suggesting the creation of a "committee of color" to make sure all members and office holders in Congress be pure Anglo-Saxon, and to expel any member with one drop of colored blood in his veins. Or stop him from giving speeches like the one making clear that he wasn't going to talk about slavery, much in the way someone might tell you right now not to think about an elephant. (That's right. An elephant. Don't think of one.) Or asking those congressmen who described slavery as a positive good for slaves to please explain in some detail to somewhat obtuse Northerners like himself just how that could be.[9]

In some sense, of course, JQA's campaign did little good. Sure, it irritated proslavery advocates in ways that even their Northern allies found secretly amusing, but it didn't change the gag rule, which became permanent in 1840, literally written into the rulebook governing the House of Representatives and no longer requiring regular renewal. On the other hand, it was becoming increasingly clear the gag rule was having precisely the

opposite effect that was intended. Indeed, at times it was difficult
to discuss matters some in Congress really did want to take up. A
good example is the status of Texas, which rebelled against Mexico and became an autonomous republic in 1836. Many Americans and Texans alike wanted Texas to join the Union, and indeed
JQA himself had explored such a possibility when he was president. But by the 1830s everybody knew Texas would join the
Union as a slave state. Mexicans had originally welcomed American settlers into poorly populated areas as long as they didn't
bring their slaves, one rule among many that settlers simply ignored. Bringing Texas into the Union now was going to raise all
kinds of sticky questions the Jackson and Van Buren administrations would rather avoid. Nor were the Whigs, the party to
which Adams presumably belonged, eager to engage the issue,
which polarized the electorate. The Whigs were just as happy to
have slavery taken off the table altogether when they took control of Congress after the election of 1840.

Yet JQA still prattled on. When he tried to bring up a petition from yet more abolitionist women in 1838, Adams responded to those who asserted that females had no place in
politics with a long speech about their importance in history
from the time of the Old Testament, including "Esther, who by a
*PETITION* saved her people and her country."[10] His remarks
culminated in a discussion of the role of South Carolinian
women in the American Revolution. When slaveholders tested
how far he would go by sending him what they considered outra-
geous petitions, he called their bluff, presenting one asking that
all free blacks be enslaved, and another that Adams be expelled
from Congress altogether as a public enemy. He even received
death threats.

And then, in January 1842, John Quincy Adams went too far:
He wanted to discuss dissolving the Union. This dramatic
proposition emerged from a serpentine parliamentary process.
The immediate context was yet another petition, again intro-
duced by Adams himself, calling for his removal from the chair-
manship of the foreign relations committee because he was
"possessed of a species of monomania on all subjects connected
with people as dark as a Mexican" and therefore could not be

trusted to deal with important issues like U.S. policy toward that country.[11] Proslavery advocates claimed this petition was a hoax and just another pretext for bringing up slavery, but Adams responded by supplying evidence that House members themselves had been discussing the idea of removing him in their own correspondence with constituents. His personal and professional competence was being called into question, he said. As such, he had a right under House rules to defend himself, and Polk reluctantly agreed.

In the process of making that defense, JQA addressed a series of petitions he had received, resulting in repeated objections from his colleagues. One of the petitions Adams referred to came from his own constituents, a group of women from Haverhill, Massachusetts. They were concerned that "a vast proportion of the resources of one section of the Union is annually drained to sustain the views and course of another section." And so they asked for legal separation.[12]

"This is a petition for the dissolution of the Union," an incredulous South Carolinian observed. Adams replied by suggesting that the petition be referred to a committee that would draft an answer to the petitioners explaining why their hopes should not be realized. Such a mild resolution was not what his opponents had in mind: Congressman Henry Wise of Virginia demanded Adams be censured for violating the gag rule for merely holding this discussion. Some Southerners had their doubts about going ahead with such a resolution, which would allow the old man to keep talking. But the vote to proceed narrowly passed. Adams was thrilled: "Good!" he said when he learned the news. He heartily voted with those who wanted to censure him.

The man designated to make the case against Adams was Thomas Marshall of Kentucky. His father, John Marshall, the legendary chief justice of the Supreme Court, had been appointed to the Supreme Court by JQA's father. More in sorrow than in anger, Marshall said that if his own father had taken seriously a petition to end the Union, his son would be obligated to do what he now did to Adams: accuse him of treason.

The charge against him was now ratcheted up, and it was JQA's turn to respond. But rather than give a speech, he asked the clerk of the House to read the first paragraph of the Declaration of Independence. Adams exhorted the hesitant clerk on until he reached this passage: "But when a long train of abuses and usurpations, pursuing invariably the same object, evinced a design to reduce them under absolute despotism, it is their right, their duty, to throw off such government."

This is the point, Adams told the House. The people have a right to seek changes. I myself don't believe we've reached the point we need to dissolve the Union, he said. But I should be able to discuss the views of those who feel we have reached that point.

Congressman Wise stood up and asked the clerk to go find Washington's famous "Farewell Address." Adams asked for a pause so that Marshall's treason charge could be printed and he have time to prepare a formal answer, but Wise plunged ahead with a speech that invoked Washington's address in order to compare the abolitionists of the 1830s to the Tories who supported England in the American Revolution. When another member asked what this somewhat less than obvious argument had to do with printing Marshall's charges and postponing the hearing, Adams himself expressed a wish that Wise "be permitted to go on." Wise did go on, making this assertion: "The principle of slavery is a leveling principle; it is friendly to equality. Break down slavery and you would with the same blow break down the great democratic principle of equality among men."

A *Congressional Globe* reporter noted that laughter was heard in the House.

In fact, there is a kind of logic to this: Freedom is a relative concept that depends on a consciousness of slavery; equality draws its meaning from an awareness, if not the actual presence, of inequality. But in this context, as in many since, Wise just sounded ridiculous. The Declaration of Independence did not say some men are created equal, it said all men are, and if that was more a wish than a reality, the desire of some proslavery advocates to make slavery an *ideal* seemed, well, un-American.

In any case, no one in that room was going to explain the intentions of the Founding Fathers to John Quincy Adams. George Washington had given him his first job in the government. Jefferson had been a frequent dinner guest in his home. He had

held important positions in the Madison and Monroe administrations. All these men were Virginians—southerners and slaveholders. But they never argued that slavery was a *good* thing.
Necessary, perhaps, but not desirable. If anything had changed in
recent years, it was not John Quincy Adams. Instead, it was the
men of the South.

> It was unexpected, most perfectly unexpected to him [here
> Adams is speaking in the third person] when he knew what
> these great men of Revolutionary times, who were Virginians,
> thought of slavery—of the institution to which now everything
> was to be sacrificed—when he now saw members from that
> State, endeavoring to destroy him and his character, for the
> sole purpose of presenting a petition. He should have hoped
> better things of Virginians.

By early February, it was clear the censure proceeding against
John Quincy Adams was becoming an embarrassment to his rivals. At one point, someone objected that during his defense
Adams had violated the gag rule, but Speaker Polk ruled in JQA's
favor. When Polk's ruling was contested, a vote was taken and it
was affirmed—the first time Adams had ever prevailed in a gagging contest. After a week of this, a Virginia Whig proposed surrender by tabling the motion against Adams. By a vote of 106–93,
the resolution was tabled. Not quite an acquittal—rather, a procedural fiction that the matter will be taken up later—but a victory nonetheless.

That victory was ambiguous but ultimately decisive in a
broader sense. In fact, the gag rule remained on the books for almost three more years. But this was a turning point, the beginning of a complex procedural process by which attempts to affirm
it prevailed by gradually smaller margins until it was finally overturned for good in December 1844. There are multiple explanations for this development. But key among them was a realization
among Northern Democrats who had been collaborating with
Southern Democrats that regional identity was becoming more
decisive than party identity. As a result of such strains, the national Whig Party would collapse entirely, and from its ashes

would emerge a Republican Party that was decisively North-ern—and antislavery.

Adams was never completely alone in the gag rule fight. William Slade of Vermont and Joshua Giddings of Michigan, for example, were stalwarts in the fight against slavery. Others, like Caleb Cushing of Massachusetts, were fellow travelers, even if their racial attitudes were not exactly what we would call enlight-ened. But from the beginning, Adams was the leader in the strug-gle. Only "Old Man Eloquent," as he was called with increasing fondness by his growing number of supporters, had the stature and cleverness to stand up consistently to his opponents. He also, again with collaboration (notably that of abolitionist Theodore Weld), articulated the most powerful rationales for fighting the gag and slavery alike, using the very states' rights logic of proslavery theorists against them. If indeed slavery was strictly a local affair, as they claimed, then freedom was, in effect, the na-tional default setting: Only with special intervention by law could slavery be created and sustained—special intervention that in many cases would require the approval and resources of nonslave states. And, as he suggested in his famous speech on the Mexican question or in the petition of those Haverhill women, such ap-proval and resources might not always be there on demand.

Above all, there was that legendary Adams will. In the aftermath of the *Amistad* case of 1839–41, in which Adams, making a rare ap-pearance before the Supreme Court, won the freedom of slaves who overpowered their Spanish captors only to be captured off Long Island Sound, made the following observation in his diary:

> The world, the flesh, and all the devils in hell are arrayed against any man who now in this North American Union shall dare to join the standard of Almighty God to put down the African slave-trade; and what can I, upon the verge of my sev-enty-fourth birthday, with a shaking hand, a darkening eye, a drowsy brain, and with all my faculties dropping by me one by one, as teeth are dropping from my head—what can I do for the cause of God and man, for the progress of human emanci-pation, for the suppression of the African slave trade? Yet my conscience presses me on; let me die upon the breach.[13]

He did. Adams collapsed on the floor of the House in February 1848 while protesting the reading of a tribute commending Mexican War veterans, because he felt the war, begun under false pretenses by now-President James Polk, had been illegal and immoral. Adams died, still in the Capitol, two days later.

In 1820, during the often frighteningly fierce debates over slavery during the Missouri Compromise, Secretary of state Adams had written, "Oh, but if one man could arise with a genius capable of comprehending, a heart capable of supporting, and an utterance capable of communicating those eternal truths that belong to this question . . . such a man would perform the duties of an angel upon the earth."[14]

Twenty-eight years later, such a man was in the House the day Adams collapsed. His seat was twenty rows behind that of Old Man Eloquent, an obscure, one-term congressman who, like Adams, also thought the Mexican War was illegal and immoral, and he would be punished by the voters back home by saying so on the record. But he had more of a common touch than Adams did, and in the end that would make all the difference. His name was Abraham Lincoln. In 1861, one of JQA's protégés, the abolitionist senator Charles Sumner of Massachusetts, visited the president-elect and outlined a hypothesis for constitutionally ending slavery during a military emergency, which he had first heard from Adams, and that Adams had outlined during the gag rule fight. The following year, Lincoln issued the Emancipation Proclamation, resting on JQA's legal logic. It is the cornerstone of Lincoln's presidential reputation.

From its awkward beginning to its embarrassing end, JQA's own presidency had been a bust, as he knew as well as anyone. However distinguished his record, he isn't as vividly remembered as his father (who also had a lousy presidency) or Lincoln, who represents the gold standard in this regard. By such measures—tough, but realistic—one would have to say that Adams the president was a failure.

But failure was the beginning, not the end, for John Quincy Adams. Dyspeptic, unyielding, and deficient in small but indispensable informal graces, he lacked the skills necessary for a successful presidency. But defeat liberated his spirit. The off-putting high-mindedness of his presidential life was transformed into an impressive sense of commitment in his congressional career. An apparent air of prickly isolation was revealed as an independent spirit of leadership. And long-held private convictions gained authority as they emerged as public causes. Adams didn't so much change his character as adapt it. In so doing, he performed crucial work in the long, hard process of making the nation adapt, too. If, in the politics of abolition, Lincoln was Jesus Christ, then Adams was John the Baptist—the prophet in the desert who defiantly insisted on spreading the good news that a better world was in view.

*(previous page)* BEYOND SHADOWS OF DOUBT: Abraham Lincoln, by Alexander Gardner, November 1863. By the time this portrait was made, Lincoln's religious beliefs, from which he had distanced himself for much of his adult life, were leading him to actively reconsider how much mastery this presumably self-made man had over his own life—and the relationship between Americans' quest for freedom and the will of an egalitarian God. (Presidential Portraits, Library of Congress)

## CHAPTER THREE

# REPRESENTATIVE LINCOLN SMEARS A PREACHER

*In which we see an ambitious politico achieve the moral—and spiritual—clarity of a great emancipator*

In 1824, a young Methodist minister named Peter Cartwright decided to give up riding the religious circuit in Kentucky and Tennessee and to settle down in Sangamon County, Illinois. In large measure he did so because he no longer wished to preach to slaveholders. Over the course of the next five decades, he became a famous and beloved preacher in his adopted state, promoting the rising tide of Methodism in the rapidly growing West. Cartwright also happened to be a passionate Democrat, combining his stern code of personal morality (no drinking, gambling, or fancy dress) with a Jacksonian hostility to big government schemes like railroads and canals promoted by the Whigs. He also railed against elitist Eastern ministers who swept through the region looking for converts—and contributions— even as they peered down on those they regarded as beneath them.

Though "Uncle Peter" was widely considered honest, with a good sense of humor, his homespun fusion of politics and religion was not universally admired. Twice elected to the state legislature, Cartwright was surprised during an 1830 campaign swing through Macon County, in the central part of the state, that a "shambling and shabbily dressed" young man in the audience challenged him on relatively abstruse points. Cartwright was astonished by "the close reasoning and the uncouth figure" of the local hired hand.

Four years later, that local hired hand, Abraham Lincoln, had himself been elected to the state legislature, and he continued to find Cartwright objectionable. This time, however, he challenged his opponent surreptitiously, writing a caustic letter to the editor of a state newspaper using a pseudonym, as he often did in these years. Cartwright, he claimed, is a hypocrite. He complains about rich Easterners who look down on Western settlers while making money off of them, but he does precisely the same thing.

> He has one of the largest and best improved farms in Sangamon county, with other property in proportion. And how has he got it? Only by the contributions he has been able to levy upon and collect from a priest ridden church. It will not do to say he has earned it "by the sweat of his brow;" for although he may sometimes labor, all know that he spends the greater part of his time in preaching and electioneering.[1]

This was a low blow. No one could legitimately consider Cartwright a carpetbagger, and comparing a Methodist minister to a (authoritarian) priest was a particularly offensive charge in a part of the world where anti-Catholic bias was strong. While he took the lead in speaking out against the evils he saw around him, Cartwright was a thoroughgoing Democrat in matters of politics, religion, and social relations.

Lincoln was playing a dangerous game, and his antics would cost him when he faced Cartwright as an opponent in an 1846 race for a seat in the U.S. House of Representatives. Cartwright, nursing a grudge, spread rumors that his Whig opponent was an infidel—a serious charge in highly religious (and heavily Democratic) Illinois. The credibility of the accusation was sufficiently threatening that Lincoln felt it necessary to circulate a handbill in response:

A charge having got into circulation in some of the neighbor-
hoods in this district, in substance that I am an open scoffer at
Christianity, I have by the advice of some friends concluded to
notice the subject in this form. That I am not a member of any
Christian church, it is true; but I have never denied the truth of
the Scriptures; and I have never spoken with intentional disre-
spect of religion in general, or of any denomination of Chris-
tians in particular. . . . I do not think I could myself, be brought
to support a man for office, whom I knew to be an open enemy
of, and scoffer at, religion.[2]

The key word, in the first and last sentences of this passage, is
"open": A *secret* scoffer at Christianity, one who anonymously
*wrote* of religion disrespectfully in the cadences of the notorious
atheist Thomas Paine, would, presumably, be another matter.
Young Abe Lincoln may have been truthful, but he wasn't exactly
honest, at least in this case.

Nor was he particularly inclined to dwell on, never mind sen-
timentalize, the kind of dirt-farmer roots Peter Cartwright ritu-
alistically celebrated. There is a rich body of anecdotal evidence
to this effect: of Lincoln himself disparaging farmwork and the
rustic circumstances of his own background, and of family and
acquaintances of his youth describing him as lazy (by which they
meant he often had his head buried in a book). But the most important statement of his priorities takes the form of action rather
than words: following two trips to New Orleans on a flatboat to
move cargo down the Mississippi River as an adolescent, Lincoln
left home for good when he was 22 years old.

In this dawn of industrial capitalism, Lincoln was eager to
begin the new day. His first real job was as a retail clerk, and after
a stint of service in the Illinois militia he started his own business.
It failed. But despite the fact that it took him years to repay his
debts, Lincoln remained a believer in what his hero, four-time
presidential candidate Henry Clay, called "The American System," the pillar of which was entrepreneurship. (Clay coined the
term "self-made man.") All through his twenties, Lincoln continued his education, and entered politics through the Illinois legislature, where he served four two-year terms. But his primary
occupation was becoming a lawyer. By his mid-thirties he was a

husband and father with a large house in the middle of the state
capital of Springfield. And by his forties he was intervening financially on behalf of improvident relatives back home—and dis-
pensing advice to them about the wisdom of leaving the farm and
taking a job in a town or city.

Like many young people who pull up stakes and go seek their
fortunes in the big city, Lincoln's actions as a young man constituted a rejection not only of his family origins, but of family
members themselves. While the particular circumstances are unclear and sometimes contested, there is general agreement that
Lincoln did not get along particularly well with his father, who
often sold his son's services to neighboring farmers and kept the
proceeds, as he was legally entitled to do until Lincoln turned 21
(something the son considered a form of slavery in its own right).
Lincoln did not invite his father to his wedding, refused to return
home during his father's final illness, and did not attend his funeral (he did, however, name a son after him following the old
man's death). Perhaps ironically, Lincoln enjoyed a notably loving relationship with the stepmother who entered his life upon
the death of his mother when he was nine years old; she was the
last person he visited before leaving for Washington after his
election as president.

More to the point at hand, Lincoln also rejected his family's
religious heritage. His parents and stepmother were Baptists.
More specifically, they were so-called hard-shell Baptists, which
meant they subscribed to the Calvinist doctrine of predestination. Responding to the Catholic practice of selling indulgences
and other rituals of man-made salvation, this doctrine, embraced
by some Congregationalist, Presbyterian, and Baptist congrega-
tions, emphasized God's complete knowledge and control over
an individual's fate. There was nothing anyone could do to alter
that fate; the best one could hope for were signs that one was
among the elect foreordained for a life in heaven.

As a child and young man, Lincoln's attitude toward this
doctrine was at best indifferent and at worst downright hostile.
He apparently refused to sing at church, and regaled his siblings
with parodies of the preachers they heard at the previous week's
service. In adulthood, he systematically studied a host of writ-

ers—Paine, Jeremy Bentham, John Stuart Mill, and others—who were militantly secular in orientation. Parthena Hill, wife of a friend in New Salem, Illinois, where Lincoln lived for much of the 1830s, once asked him, "Do you really believe there isn't any future state?" He reputedly replied, "Mrs. Hill, I'm afraid there isn't. It isn't a pleasant thing to think that when we die that is the last of us."[3]

As he got older, particularly after his race against Cartwright, Lincoln became more circumspect. Moreover, he was capable of expressing a very traditional sense of piety, even when one senses there was not much feeling behind it. As his father was dying in 1851, he wrote his stepbrother to remind Thomas Lincoln that God "notes the fall of a sparrow, and numbers the hairs of our heads; and He will not forget the dying man, who puts his trust in Him,"[4] eliding the question of whether Lincoln himself put his trust in the Lord. At the urging of his wife, he rented a pew at an Old School (i.e., Calvinist) Presbyterian Church after the death of one of his sons in 1852. But he never formally joined that or any other church.

As many observers have noted, the evangelical variety of Christianity that swept the United States in the first half of the nineteenth century meshed well with the advent of industrial capitalism, notably in the value both placed on individual striving. Notwithstanding its emphasis on spiritual predestination, Calvinism also fostered the pursuit of secular upward mobility; the Puritan work ethic, in which believers labored on earth for signs of heavenly salvation, is a case in point. Lincoln was never an evangelical, and he apparently jettisoned much of the faith of his fathers. But if anything, casting aside such baggage only made it easier to embrace the civil religion of upward mobility so central to his experiences and worldview.

There was, however, a real complication in that civil religion, one that became more obvious, even insistent, by the middle of his life: the institution of slavery. No reality of American life so insistently defined the gap between national ideals and realities. One could argue that unlike his religious background, slavery was a relatively remote issue for Lincoln. After all, he was not a slaveholder, and he lived in a state where slavery was illegal (though various transit laws and legal irregularities made slavery a reality even in Illinois). But always, it loomed in the background.

For virtually his entire life, Lincoln's position was consistent: He hated slavery but believed it had to be tolerated where it already existed. This stance is captured most vividly and concisely in a deeply engaged letter he wrote to his best friend, Joshua Speed, in 1855. "You may remember, as I well do," he wrote of a steamboat trip the two took fourteen years earlier, "there were, on board, ten or a dozen slaves, shacked together with various irons. That sight was a continual torment to me. . . . It is hardly fair for you to assume that I have no interest in a thing which has, and continually exercises, the power of making me miserable. You ought rather appreciate how much the great body of Northern people do crucify their feelings, in order to maintain their loyalty to the constitution and the Union."[5]

There was another reason for Lincoln's willingness to "crucify" his feelings: his belief that slavery was contained in the South and would eventually die out. In this regard, he was not an abolitionist, but rather an extinctionist. By drawing a line that ran west from the northern Arkansas border, the Missouri Compromise of 1820 had limited the possibility of new slave states north of Kentucky—Missouri was, by definition, the exception. And what politicians could not prevent, nature would: The landscape and climate of the Midwest and Great Plains did not lend themselves to plantation agriculture. Under such circumstances, it did not make sense to inflame the issue, however personally satisfying it may have been for high-minded moralists to denounce slavery. Far better, Lincoln felt, to convey a sense of respect, even sympathy, for slave owners, many of whom no doubt felt compelled by custom and competition to participate in an unjust system. So, for example, while Lincoln was only one of a handful of Illinois legislators who signed a statement he co-authored protesting a set of resolutions condemning abolitionist societies in 1837, that statement added that "the promulgation of abolition doctrines tends rather to increase than to abate" the evils of slavery.[6]

While his stance had real plausibility as a strategy for ending slavery, it may well be that its chief beneficiary was Lincoln himself. In effect, it allowed him to get on with his political life with something resembling a good conscience. After defeating Cartwright in 1846, he took his seat in Congress the following year just as the Mexican War—a war launched on dubious claims of foreign aggression, and undertaken with thinly veiled hopes for expanding slavery—was getting underway. An appalled Lincoln gave an impassioned speech denouncing the administration of James K. Polk. Nobody in Washington paid much notice, but the voters back in Illinois weren't happy with their congressman, even though Lincoln (like Democratic presidential candidate John Kerry in 2004) voted for financial support to the troops in a cause he disliked. Damaged by his opposition to what turned out to be a quick and hugely successful war, Lincoln relinquished his seat, which went to the Democrats. When his wife refused to abide an offer for Lincoln to become the governor of the new territory of Oregon, he had nowhere to go but home. For the next few years (1850–54), he prospered as a high-priced litigator, but he was widely perceived, and felt himself to be, a man who had come a long way, but had not gone nearly as far as he might have—as far, for example, as his lifetime rival Stephen Douglas, who came up through the ranks of the Illinois legislature, got elected to the U.S. Senate, and was now discussed as obvious presidential timber.

One of the great ironies of Lincoln's career is that his star began to rise in the 1850s only after he engaged the slavery controversy that he and most of his fellow politicians had spent most of their careers avoiding. Lincoln was always a pragmatist on the slavery question. But he never failed to cast the matter in moral terms. Lincoln regarded Stephen Douglas's advocacy of "popular sovereignty"—i.e., allowing the voters of a territory to decide whether or not to allow slavery—as callous indifference masquerading as democratic principle. In the last of his celebrated seven debates with Douglas for a U.S. Senate seat in 1858, Lincoln put the matter in admirably plain terms:

> It is the struggle between two principles—right and wrong—throughout the world. They are the two principles that have stood face to face from the beginning of time; and will ever

continue to struggle. The one is the common right of human-
ity and the other is the divine right of kings. It is the spirit that
says, "You work and toil and earn bread, and I'll eat it." No
matter in what shape it comes, whether from the mouth of a
king who seeks to bestride the people of his own nation and
live by the fruit of their labor, or from one race of man as an
apology for enslaving another race, it is the same tyrannical
principle.[7]

Lincoln lost that election, but the position he staked out—
asserting both the essential evil of slavery and the essential necessity of the Union—became the basis of the governing
coalition that brought him to the presidency in 1860. The ten-
sile balance between morality and politics in his public life was
paralleled in his inner life, where he saw no fundamental conflict
between morality and ambition. So fortified, he stepped into the
whirlwind.

It is perhaps a truism of aging that the very things one rejects
from one's childhood have a way of returning in some form,
often unexpectedly. So it was with Lincoln's religious beliefs. The
rebellious spirit of youth gave way to circumspection in middle
age. But even here, there were signs that he never quite surrendered his Calvinist heritage. In the very statement of the 1846
congressional campaign against Cartwright, in which he said he
while never support an open scoffer at religion, Lincoln noted
that he was raised in a predestinarian household, and that he had
since sometimes maintained this point of view—privately—he
had not done so in years. It nevertheless lurks as a subtext in the
moving farewell address he gave to friends and neighbors in
Springfield as he left to become president in 1861. Lincoln noted
that he faced a challenge even more daunting than that which
faced Washington, and headed to the nation's capital not knowing whether he would ever return (he did not). "Without the assistance of that Divine Being, who ever attended him, I cannot
succeed. With that assistance I cannot fail," he said.[8] Perhaps not

surprisingly, this invocation of divine will has much more imme-
diacy and sincerity than the detached message he had written to
his father a decade earlier.

As president, Lincoln would invoke God's name with an un-
selfconsciousness and sincerity that is perceptively more earnest
than earlier in his life. Nowhere is this new engagement with religious matters—and, more specifically, his hard-shell Baptist religious background—more significant than the most important
act of Lincoln's career: the Emancipation Proclamation. As was
true of many of the difficult decisions Lincoln made in his public
life, he vetted a variety of opinions on the matter, and played
devil's advocate with those he agreed with as well as those he did
not without tipping his hand. He also wrestled with difficult
questions via private writings he made to clarify his thinking. So,
for example, in early September of 1862—mere days before issuing the Proclamation on September 17—he wrote, "The will of
God prevails. I am almost ready to say this is probably true—that
God wills this contest, and wills that it shall not end yet." Almost,
but not quite: Lincoln still saw himself as an agent of his own
(and the nation's) destiny. A week after issuing the Proclamation
Lincoln told a crowd of serenaders who had gathered to celebrate that "I can only trust in God that I have made no
mistake. . . . It is now for the country and the world to pass judgment on it."⁹

As time went on, however, Lincoln's Calvinist heritage became ever more apparent—and ever more entwined with his understanding of his role in the ending of slavery. This linkage is
clear in Lincoln's famous 1864 letter to Kentucky newspaper editor Albert Hodges, who had come with a delegation to the White
House to complain about Lincoln's decision to abandon his campaign pledge not to interfere with slavery where it already existed, and in particular to arm African Americans to fight in the
Civil War. Lincoln ended the letter with a striking assertion that
his intentions in the matter were beside the point: "I do not claim
to control events, but confess plainly that events have controlled
me. Now, at the end of three years struggle the nation's condition
is not what either party, or any man devised, or expected. God
alone can claim it. Whether it is tending is plain. If God now

wills the removal of a great wrong, and wills also that we of the North as well as you of the South, shall pay fairly for our complicity in that wrong, impartial history will find therein new cause to attest and revere the justice and goodness of God."[10]

One might think that the most decisive ramification of believing that all is in God's hands would be passivity. But the Calvinism of the Puritans only seemed to impel a greater sense of purpose in the hope that a work ethic was a sign, however faint, of election. In Lincoln's case, however, the outcome was compassion. His law partner William Herndon, who called him a "thorough fatalist," described Lincoln as a man who believed that no one was finally responsible for one's actions, resulting in "charity for men and his want of malice for them everywhere."[11] There is a great deal of anecdotal and even documented evidence for this view: Lincoln's reputed reluctance to hurt animals; his notable leniency in dealing with deserters; even his mild reaction to the machinations of former rivals, many of them in his own cabinet, who disparaged him publicly and privately.

This view of life also had an increasingly decisive impact on Lincoln's view of race relations. "Suppose it is true," he wrote to himself around the time of the Lincoln-Douglas debates, "that the negro is inferior to the white, in the gifts of nature; is it not just the exact reverse justice that white should, for that reason, take from the negro, any part of the little which has been given him? 'Give to him that is needy,' is the Christian rule of charity; but 'Take from him that is needy' is the rule of slavery."[12] Even as he stipulates white supremacy, Lincoln's logic moves him toward equality.

Perhaps the supreme expression of Lincoln's egalitarian spirit was his Second Inaugural, in which, unlike his First Inaugural, he foregrounds slavery as a cause of the war but does so in characteristically humble terms. Noting that both North and South invoked the Lord to aid their causes, he noted, "It may seem strange that any men should ask a just God's assistance in wringing their bread from the sweat of other men's faces, but let us not judge that we be not judged." In any case, he suggested in cadences reminiscent of the Hodges letter, that the Civil War was the Lord's punishment to North *and* South for the sin of slavery, a punishment that will be meted out in God's time and on God's terms. The most important thing Americans can do now, he said, is show malice toward none, charity for all, and, with firmness in the right, "as God gives us to see the right," care for the veteran, the widow, and the orphan. We are not to claim God for our side, but to place ourselves on God's side. The most worthy ambition was to exercise our freedom by choosing to accept His will.[13]

On March 4, 1865, the legendary political fixer Thurlow Weed, who had once backed Lincoln's former rival (and now close friend) Secretary of state William Seward, wrote the president a letter congratulating him on a recent speech formally acknowledging his reelection. Lincoln mistakenly believed Weed was complimenting him on his Second Inaugural, for which he was especially grateful to receive praise, because he suspected "it is not immediately popular. Men are not flattered by being shown that there has been a difference between the Almighty and them. To deny it, however, in this case, is to deny that there is a God governing the world. It is a truth which I thought needed to be told; and as whatever of humiliation there is in it, falls most directly on myself, I thought others might afford for me to tell it."[14]

The great American historian Richard Hofstadter, not a man with much sympathy, or even patience, for religious enthusiasm (nor, for that matter, the degree of what he considered personal calculation that went into young Mr. Lincoln's political ambitions), once wrote that "here perhaps is the best measure of Lincoln's personal eminence in the human calendar—that he was chastened and not intoxicated by power."[15] The proud, maybe even insolent, young man in shabby clothes who took on the Reverend Peter Cartwright had accomplished about as much as any mere mortal ever has. Yet at the very pinnacle of his career he testified to a powerful sense of earned humility. Whatever we choose to believe about a Kingdom of Heaven beyond this earthly republic, here, truly, is an example of leadership to follow.

# "GENTLEMAN BOSS" ARTHUR BITES THE HAND THAT FEEDS HIM

*In which we see a political hack realize
the virtues of good governance*

"The Ohio men have offered me the vice-presidency," Chester Alan Arthur told New York senator Roscoe Conkling.[1] This was not welcome news. Arthur had long been Conkling's protégé, and perhaps under other circumstances Conkling, the chief fixer of the so-called Stalwart[2] faction of the Republican Party, would have accepted the prospect of an Arthur vice presidency with enthusiasm. But Conkling—the dapper, silver-tongued epicurean with a firm grip on the levers of party discipline—had been working for months to secure the presidential nomination for former president Ulysses S. Grant, and to quash the aspirations of his archrival, James Blaine of Maine, leader of the so-called Half-Breed faction. The back-room deadlock at the Republican National Convention in Chicago led, as convention deadlocks so often did in those days, to a search for an acceptable compromise candidate, and James

Garfield of Ohio had emerged as that figure in Chicago in June of 1880.

The Garfield contingent at the convention, hoping to build a bridge to the Stalwarts, offered the vice presidential slot to Levi P. Morton, a New Yorker and a Conkling ally. But Conkling, still smarting at Grant's defeat, told Morton to refuse the position, because Conkling was not willing to be mollified by what he considered a token gesture. When Morton did, the New York delegation at the convention approached the Garfield camp and indicated they'd like to see another one of their own, Chester Alan Arthur, as VP, and the offer was tendered to Arthur directly. This second choice for the second slot made Conkling no happier. What he really wanted was the power to sell the most lucrative jobs in a Garfield administration, a matter that had not yet been broached. By comparison, the vice presidency was a useless bauble. It was also a matter of some irritation to Conkling that the offer had not been proffered for his consideration first, and that he was only hearing about it now. This was no way to treat the boss of the Republican Party.

"You should drop it as you would a red hot shoe from the forge," Conkling instructed Arthur.

Arthur sought to reassure the Senator. "I sought you to consult, not—"

"What is there to consult about?" Conkling snapped. "This trickster of Mentor [Garfield's hometown in Ohio] will be defeated before the country."

"There is something else to be said."

"What, sir, you think of accepting?"

Arthur paused before continuing. "The office of the vice president is a greater honor than I ever dreamed of attaining," he told Conkling. "A barren nomination would be a great honor. In a calmer moment you will look at this differently."

"If you wish for my favor and respect you will contemptuously decline it."

Arthur stiffened. "Senator Conkling, I shall accept the nomination and I shall carry with me a majority of the delegates."

Speechless, Conkling glared at Arthur. He turned and left the room.

Arthur may have stood up to Conkling and satisfied his vanity by accepting the second slot on the ticket, but most observers were not impressed. The most memorable estimation of Arthur's selection came from E. L. Godkin, editor of the *Nation*. "There is no place in which his powers of mischief will be so small as in the Vice Presidency," the famed political insider wrote. "General Garfield [Garfield, like his running mate, was a Civil War veteran], if elected, may die during his term of office, but that is too unlikely a contingency to be worth making extraordinary provisions for."[3]

In any event, Conkling made it clear that no VP slot was going to be sufficient to buy his support—and everybody knew that Garfield had no chance of winning the election unless he won New York. Garfield reluctantly came East to cut a deal with Conkling, who mysteriously failed to show up for their meeting. Arthur and the other Republican senator from New York, Thomas Platt, nevertheless negotiated an agreement with Garfield that would give Conkling some say over cabinet positions and patronage in a Garfield White House in exchange for Stalwart support.

Or so they believed. The Stalwarts did back Garfield, who did get elected. But while a number of Conkling men were named to government posts, Garfield named Conkling's enemy, Blaine, secretary of state. He also defied Conkling's wishes and refused to name the one-time VP prospect Morton secretary of treasury, by virtue of which he would have had the power to name the customs collector for the Port of New York. As the office responsible for receiving tax revenue from foreign shipping entering the nation's largest port, this was the most lucrative job in the federal government, with multiple opportunities, many of them dubiously legal, for officials to enrich themselves. (It was the post in which Conkling had once installed Arthur, who served as a loyal, and relatively honest, functionary, until forced out by charges of corruption among his staff.) In naming his own man, Garfield asserted that he had only agreed to consult with the Stalwarts, not take orders from them.

By the time Garfield named a Conkling opponent, William Robertson, as customs collector of New York in early 1881, there was open warfare between Conkling and the new administration. Conkling publicly declared his opposition to the Robertson nomination, mobilizing Platt and other allies for the fight. Garfield retaliated by withdrawing five Conkling men from positions for which they had been slated. Conkling and Platt raised the ante by resigning from the Senate, confident that their ability to engineer their own quick reelections (by the state legislature, which chose senators until 1913) would be a resounding rebuke of the president.

There are a number of ways to view Chester Alan Arthur's behavior through this whole imbroglio of 1880–81, none of them particularly favorable. While one cannot necessarily fault him for wanting, even accepting, the nomination for the vice presidency of the United States, it is also an axiom of politics (among other things) that, in the words of the old saying, "you dance with the girl who brung ya." Arthur owed a good deal of his considerable status to Conkling, who clearly did not want him to take the nomination.

Once the nomination became an outright election, Arthur became an embarrassment to Republicans of all stripes. At a pre-inauguration testimonial dinner, a drunken vice president–elect had appalled many observers by joking in front of reporters that "if I should get to going about secrets of the campaign, there is no saying what I might say."[4] Arthur implied, among other things, that Republicans had resorted to buying votes in Indiana.

In any event, questions about his personal or partisan loyalties should have been resolved once Arthur assumed office: His obligations were now to President Garfield. This was not only a matter of personal propriety, but of Constitutional conduct as well. The expectation—at least since the Twelfth Amendment, a response to the disastrous Adams-Jefferson split during the Adams administration—is that the vice president serves the interests of the chief executive. Arthur, however, continued to operate as a creature of Conkling through the whole Robertson controversy, publicly and privately seeking to persuade President Garfield to satisfy the Boss. When Conkling resigned from the Senate, Arthur went to Albany to campaign for his reelection, making abundantly clear where his loyalties lay. But the Conkling-Platt scheme hit a snag when Platt was caught having sex with a woman who wasn't his wife, generating a national scandal. Platt had to step aside, but the fight was by no means over.

On July 2, 1881, the day Platt withdrew from the Senate race, President Garfield walked arm in arm with Secretary of state Blaine through Washington's Baltimore & Ohio train station. Garfield was headed to New England for a summer vacation. A man named Charles J. Guiteau—almost universally described as "a disappointed office seeker," though he was clearly insane— walked up behind the president, shot him twice, and shouted, "I am a Stalwart and now Arthur is President!"[5]

Well, not quite "now." Garfield lingered for over two months, and might well have recovered had not doctors' clumsy attempts to remove the bullet infected the wound in his abdomen. Arthur, appalled by the assassination attempt, left Conkling and returned home to New York. Summoned to Washington by the cabinet, he kept as low a profile as was possible and returned home when it appeared the president would recover. When, instead, Garfield finally died on September 19, Arthur wept alone in his library. He regarded his ascension to the presidency as a "calamity." This opinion was not his alone. In the words of an acquaintance who learned Garfield was dead, "Chet Arthur? President of the United States? Good God!"[6]

Roscoe Conkling carried the new president's bags to the train station when he left New York for Washington. It was a gesture that suggested the powerful cross-currents in their relationship. Arthur, once the minion of "Lord Roscoe," had—officially, at least—catapulted past him. Moreover, Garfield's death had thrown Conkling's own plans into disarray: The New York legislature had declined to reelect him to the Senate. Still, Conkling regarded this as a temporary setback (he did, in fact, ultimately return there), and with Arthur in the White House, virtually everyone assumed the Stalwarts would control the government agenda. Perhaps no one was more confident about Arthur's orientation than Conkling. As one newspaper correspondent noted, Conkling "had been in the habit of patronizing Mr. Arthur, and had given him political orders for so many years that he could not imagine this pleasure-loving, easy-going man capable of rebellion."[7]

But Arthur was in fact capable. The first sign that this pleasure-loving, easy-going man had changed emerged about a month later, when Conkling came to Washington for a private meeting with Arthur. It was widely believed the two were conferring about a new cabinet, but it gradually became apparent that it had been a stormy session. The chief sticking point was Arthur's refusal to dismiss Garfield's appointee, Robertson, as collector of the New York customhouse—the very appointment that had been such a bone of contention between Garfield and Conkling, and one in which Arthur had taken Conkling's side. Nor did Arthur accept Conkling's advice for treasury secretary. Fuming, Conkling stormed out of the meeting, swearing that Arthur had betrayed him. Not even an appeal from Conkling's mistress helped.

Thus did the Conkling-Arthur alliance end. Arthur later made a pro forma offer to nominate Conkling, a position as justice of the Supreme Court, but Conkling refused. He never regained his influence, control of his faction passing to Platt. James Blaine, for his part, left the State Department early in the Arthur administration, planning his own bid for the presidency. Thus it was that Arthur found himself liberated from his party's two chief competitors. He could, if he chose, chart a new course.

And he did. One symbolic indication was the White House itself, which underwent a dramatic transformation. Arthur's beloved wife Ellen died shortly before he assumed the vice presidency, and he brought in his younger sister to run the household and help raise his young daughter. He also hired Louis Tiffany to overhaul the White House furnishings. The White House of Garfield's predecessor, Rutherford B. Hayes, had been a fairly staid affair, but Arthur brought liquor and opulent meals back to the residence. He also ordered a fancy new carriage to squire him about town. In rearranging the trappings of his office to match his elegant tastes, Arthur conveyed a message that he would be his own man.

On the policy front, Arthur issued two vetoes that demonstrated his fledging political independence. The first involved wading into the murky waters of race relations. In April of 1882, an alliance between Southern and Western racist congressmen resulted in the Anti-Chinese Immigration Bill, which would prevent the Chinese from entering the United States entirely for twenty years. Arthur objected to its requirement that Chinese residents already in the United States register with the federal government, and asserted that the Chinese played an important role in American economic development. Many Californians were outraged, and Arthur was burned in effigy in cities and towns throughout the West. An attempt to pass the bill over Arthur's veto failed. When it became clear that a compromise measure limiting the exclusion to ten years would pass over his veto, Arthur signed it. He could not entirely resist what he called "a breach of our national faith," but he at least mitigated it. Arthur also stood up to Congress that summer when he was presented with a so-called Rivers and Harbors Bill. The proposed legislation was a spectacular example of pork-barrel politics and Arthur again refused to accept it. He acknowledged the value of improving navigation by dredging rivers, lakes, and the coasts, but believed that this particular bill failed to do so in a fair and efficient way. Reformers were elated; Republicans were baffled and angry; Democrats plotted to exploit the disarray by gaining in midterm elections. Indeed, the 1882 returns showed a distinct shift toward the Democrats.

But the most important move Arthur made during his presidency—the only one for which he is really remembered—was to take a stand in favor Civil Service reform. This was an important and consequential decision in its own right. But it was all the more striking for its renunciation of his political way of life.

At the center of this way of life was the American party system. Political parties were important for the ideological cohesion and electoral organization they offered to members and to the electorate at large. But their core function was patronage—jobs that were controlled and distributed by party leaders who managed urban, county, and state-wide "machines." This "spoils system," which emerged decisively during Andrew Jackson's presidency in the 1830s, was an accepted fact of American politics for much of the century. By the 1880s, it was largely taken for granted that party bosses would reward loyalists with jobs regardless of their qualifications, and that the recipients of these jobs would demonstrate their gratitude by kicking back some portion of their salary ("assessments") to their party, which would in turn use the money to fuel future electoral conquests. The system may not have been pretty—indeed, by the 1870s there were increasingly vocal voices calling for reform—but it was effective in mobilizing large numbers of people to participate in the political process at a variety of levels.

Chester Alan Arthur was the quintessential product of machine politics. He had joined the Republican Party in upstate New York at the time of its formation out of abolitionist convictions, and got his first job in government as part of the ceremonial military staff of the governor—a position that became a good deal less ceremonial when the Civil War broke out and Arthur suddenly had responsibilities as assistant quartermaster general for the state, in charge of feeding, equipping and transporting thousands of New York soldiers. After the war, he came into the orbit of Roscoe Conkling, who would soon emerge as a leading lieutenant of President Ulysses S. Grant, and the power broker of New York state politics. It was in deference to Conkling, and in recognition of Arthur's usefully clean reputation, that President Grant appointed Arthur as collector of the Port of New York with responsibility for supervising vast amounts of money and control over more than a thousand government employees. It was during these years that Arthur cemented his reputation as the "Gentleman Boss," known for his tact, refinement, and desire to please superior and subordinate alike. The temptation for corruption in the position was almost irresistible, but there is widespread agreement that Arthur himself remained honest, even if not all his underlings were, and even if his payroll was padded.

By this point, however, it was not quite enough for government servants to not be active felons. A new generation of reformers was struggling to come of age in American life, arguing that patronage politics was no longer acceptable in a nation of growing size and complexity—that bona fide occupational qualifications, not political connections, should be the primary consideration in determining who got which jobs. Among other things, they argued, candidates for government jobs should be required to pass tests that documented their competence to perform the tasks required for satisfactory service. These reformers were joined by a chorus of Democrats and even some Republicans, who called for changes at the New York customhouse, particularly as an investigation showed mounting evidence of fraud on the part of one of Arthur's deputies. Eventually the new (Half-Breed) Republican president, Rutherford B. Hayes—who, not coincidentally, was no fan of Conkling's—forced Arthur out in 1877.

By 1880, when the Garfield-Arthur ticket captured the presidency, the notion of Civil Service reform had become appealing enough that politicians of all stripes paid lip service to the idea. Arthur himself had indicated support for reform during the campaign, though he expressed deep reservations about the idea of competitive examinations. This combination of vague support coupled by opposition to essential provisions characterized the overall discussion surrounding the proposal of Democratic Ohio senator George Pendleton's reform bill. It had gone nowhere.

But Arthur was deeply shaken by the fact that he became president, in effect, over a question of patronage. Garfield's assassin was a frustrated office-seeker. It didn't matter that he was never remotely a candidate for the post of United States ambassador to France that he believed God wanted him to have. Actually, his attorney would unsuccessfully use the new defense of insanity for his client, who was sentenced to death. Arthur allowed for a last-minute appeal, but refused to overturn the sentence. He was, however, determined to redeem his predecessor's death.

Upon assuming the presidency, Arthur stunned observers by announcing a much more affirmative position on Civil Service reform than he previously had, even if he didn't go much beyond that. The idea got further momentum in the midterm elections of 1882, which suggested a restless mood in the country. Pendleton's bill got a new lease on life, though the politics of the measure were such that the Democrats, who sensed a takeover of the federal government—all those jobs!—was in the offing, and were thus generally less enthusiastic than Republicans. The bill nevertheless passed both houses of Congress. Arthur decided to go with the flow of reform rather than impede the tide and signed it into law in January of 1883.

Considered in isolation, the Pendleton Act was hardly much of a reform. Democrats had watered down many of its provisions, and at its inception the law only covered 10 percent of federal jobs (among them customs houses, like New York's, with more than fifty employees). Nevertheless, the law established an important precedent, and the number of jobs covered by its provisions expanded rapidly. Enforcement lay with the executive branch, and Arthur responded with commissioners who were warmly endorsed by reformers. While political appointees continue to dominate many government positions to this day, a basic shift in expectations had occurred that would last for about a century. That Chester Alan Arthur, a man whose entire career had been premised on party patronage, would sign such a law is a testament to his fundamental integrity—and his ability to grow in office.

There was a price to be paid for such growth, however. By the start of the 1884 campaign, Arthur was in a sense a man without a party. He would have liked to stand for reelection, but had alienated his base among the Stalwarts. And while he had surprised and impressed some reformers, many remained skeptical and were in any case hardly in a position to confer many votes on him. After a perfunctory expression of support in the first ballot at the Republican National Convention, the Half-Breed-dominated party rallied around Blaine. Blaine ultimately lost the presidential election to Democrat Grover Cleveland, the only Democrat to occupy the White House in the half-century between the presidencies of Abraham Lincoln and Woodrow Wilson. (He was also the only president to win two nonconsecutive terms, returning to office after the election of 1892.)

Arthur, for his part, had never particularly hankered for reelection in the first place. There was always a sense of hollowness in his appointment to the presidency in that he was unable to share it with his wife, who had died on the cusp of the vice presidency. His sedentary lifestyle, which included an unusually large number of state dinners at the White House, had contributed to Bright's Disease, a kidney disorder. Arthur hid his malady as much as possible from the American public, and tried to escape a White House he found dreary by traveling widely, including an extended tour of the West (he had a relatively enlightened view of Indian relations, his policies anticipating the well-intentioned, though problematic, approach of the 1887 Dawes Act, which fostered an assimilationist approach toward Native Americans). In many ways a politically and even intellectually limited man, Arthur had made the most of his opportunities with a sense of proportion and modesty that have worn well, if quietly, with time. He died in New York in 1885, about a year and a half after leaving office.

Thomas Jefferson managed to suspend his normal ideological tendencies and secured the greatest achievement of his presidency in the Louisiana Purchase. John Quincy Adams redirected his essential iconoclasm and realized his greatest achievement after his presidency in the gag rule fight. And Abraham Lincoln reconnected with his submerged religious character in the process of abolishing slavery. But Chester Alan Arthur represents a different side to this story by doing that rarest of things: He truly changed. Always the gentleman, always committed to a Republican approach to policy questions (insofar as political ideology ever mattered in his world), he nevertheless decided after becoming president that good government mattered above all else—including the chance, however remote, for a future in presidential politics. This is clear in the stand he took in favor of the Pendleton Act, but that stand was part of a larger whole that upheld fairness in questions of race relations and the economy rather than party or factional interest. Alas, it took the death of a colleague to shock Arthur into this transformation. But others have done a good deal less in the wake of substantially more. It would be a mistake to call Chester Alan Arthur a great president. But it would also be a mistake to overlook his achievement.

(*previous page*) STRADDLING THE GLOBE: Theodore Roosevelt, 1903. Nothing about TR was modest, but his arrogance was arrogated for democratic ends. A product of affluence, he had nothing but contempt for mere money—and those who believed that it entitled them to special privilege. (Presidential Portraits, Library of Congress)

CHAPTER FIVE

# DUDE T.R. ENTERS THE ARENA

*In which we see an imperial democrat*
*reveal that impatience can be a virtue*

The most ridiculous debut in modern American politics occurred on the evening of January 2, 1882, at the Capitol in Albany, New York, where the Republican caucus of the New York State Assembly gathered for the new legislative session. There were 128 members in the Assembly—61 Republicans, 59 regular Democrats, and 8 members of the Tammany Democratic machine of New York City, ready to cast their lot with the highest bidder. Political gridlock loomed, but the Republicans at least wanted to settle on the renomination of the House Speaker, Thomas Alvord, on the night before the regular session began.

The caucus had largely gathered when a young man—at 23, the youngest in the Assembly—burst through the door of the chamber. He paused, allowing the gathering to take him in before proceeding. There are multiple accounts of this grand entrance, but the recollections forty years later of Assemblyman John Walsh are particularly vivid:

Suddenly our eyes, and those of everybody on the floor, became glued on a young man who was coming in through the door. His hair was parted in the center, and he had sideburns. He wore a single eye-glass, with a gold chain over his ear. He had on a cutaway coat with one button at the top, and the ends of its tails almost reached the tops of his shoes. He carried a gold-headed cane in one hand, a silk hat in the other, and he walked in the bent-over fashion that was the style of young men of the day. His trousers were as tight as a tailor could make them, and had a bell-shaped bottom to cover his shoes.

"Who's the dude?" I asked another member, while the same question was being put in a dozen different parts of the hall.

"That's Theodore Roosevelt of New York," he answered.

It was, no doubt, meant to be an impressive entrance—but that impression wasn't exactly what he intended. In the days that followed, Theodore Roosevelt acquired a series of nicknames, among them "Young Squirt," "Punkin-Lily," and "Jane Dandy." Old Tom Alvord, who had been speaker in the Assembly the day Roosevelt was born, described him as a "damn fool." He described Republican strength in the Assembly as "sixty one and one-half members."[1]

Roosevelt responded to such sarcasm sharply. "Big John" MacManus, an ex-prizefighter and Tammany man, reacted to Roosevelt's sideburns by proposing to toss "that damned dude" in a blanket. Roosevelt went up to MacManus, who towered over him, and said he had heard what MacManus said. "By God," Roosevelt snarled, "If you try anything like that I'll kick you, I'll bite you, I'll kick you in the balls, I'll do anything to you—you better leave me alone." MacManus backed off. When J. J. Costello, another Tammany member, mocked the pea coat Roosevelt wore to an Albany saloon—"Won't Mamma's boy catch cold?" he reputedly asked—Roosevelt decked him. "Now go over there and wash yourself. When you are in the presence of gentlemen, conduct yourself like a gentleman." Roosevelt later summed up the incident by saying, "I'm not going to have an Irishman or anybody else insult me."[2] (Irishmen, apparently, were a singularly insulting breed.)

For the most part Roosevelt managed to focus his volcanic energy on legislative battles. Within 48 hours of his appointment to a committee on cities, he introduced four bills—one to purify New York's water supply, another to reform the election of aldermen, a third to cancel all stocks and bonds in the city's sinking fund, and a fourth to lighten the docket of the Court of Appeals. Only one, the aldermen bill, actually passed, but that was hardly reason to be discouraged.

Yet here he was hardly less ridiculous. "Mister Spee-kar! Mister Spee-kar!" he would shout repeatedly in his Harvard accent, leaning so far forward across his desk that he risked falling over it. When an elevated railroad bill he supported was voted down without debate two months later, he insisted on reporting it anyway to embarrass his opponents, wielding a broken chair-leg at the Democrats who threatened to riot in response. Such antics resulted in a visit from railroad lobbyists, who suggested that an older and more experienced assemblyman might be more effective in this particular case, and Roosevelt agreed to having its fate taken out of his hands. Two weeks later, the bill became law.

Of course, it only became law because the lobbyists had bought its support from recalcitrant legislators. That's just the way things worked. No one, not even a young blue-blooded punk two years out of Harvard, could successfully take on the System single-handedly.

Not yet, anyway.

While he would shed the callowness (though not the penchant for drama) that marked his entry into American politics, the contours of Theodore Roosevelt's ideology were vividly defined in the three years he spent in the New York legislature. Like his father, who had served in the Lincoln administration, Roosevelt was a reformer, and embraced classic causes like closing sweatshops and imposing safeguards for working women and children. Yet the moralist in him would not go for measures to improve the conditions of prison inmates, and he had a lifelong skepticism, even hostility, toward any kind of collective action on the part of industrial workers, whom he felt were often motivated by mere envy in trying to restrain genuine hard work and innovation. At the same time, while TR knew and even admired rich industrialists, it was perhaps the single most important article of faith in his worldview that mere money should not be enough to give a man a say in how the government worked. Thus it was in describing the alleged attempt of robber baron Jay Gould to corrupt a New York State supreme court judge that TR denounced "that most dangerous of all dangerous classes, the wealthy criminal class."[3] Paradoxically, this old-money snobbery toward the nouveau riche led him to seek out and understand—master—the arts of democracy. By the mid-1880s, it was already clear to Republican party bosses that however obnoxious he might be, Roosevelt had undeniable gifts for electioneering and publicity.

That's why, despite their misgivings, they turned to him repeatedly for decades to come. By the mid-1890s, mainline Republican leaders like Thomas Platt, who had replaced Roscoe Conkling as the Boss of New York, detested Roosevelt, as did the famed national political operative Mark Hanna. (Even family members could find him exasperating. "When Theodore attends a wedding," a relative complained, "he wants to be the bride, and when he attends a funeral, he wants to be the corpse.")[4] Yet his electoral magic proved irresistible in 1896 when Roosevelt stumped for William McKinley in his presidential race against the Democratic populist William Jennings Bryan, whom TR considered an unrealistic kook—what some regarded as the pot calling the kettle black.

Reluctantly rewarded with the post of assistant secretary of the Navy—the only department in the cabinet that would find room for him—Roosevelt sidestepped the passive, vacation-prone secretary, John Long, and exercised every opportunity to issue orders, impose reforms, and generally raise the profile of the nation's maritime forces. In the aftermath of the explosion of the U.S.S. *Maine* in early 1898, an event attributed to a Spanish plot, Roosevelt took advantage of a one-day absence by Long to order the U.S. fleet to take position off the coast of the Philippines, where it would be able to bottle up the Spanish fleet in the event of war. When war did come, this proved to be a crucial strategic move, and the Spanish were in effect hobbled before they could even get out of the gate.

Roosevelt considered the Spanish-American War the opportunity of a lifetime. Born too late for the Civil War, desperate for the chance to prove his manhood in battle, the 39-year-old father of six quit his job, got himself commissioned as a colonel, and formed a regiment comprised of Harvard Ivy Leaguers and Dakota cowboys he dubbed "the Rough Riders." He arrived in Cuba that summer and demonstrated flamboyant valor in charging Spanish lines at engagements at Kettle and San Juan Hill, returning home a bona fide war hero.

His next step was the governorship of New York, which he won in 1899. Upon taking office, he launched an ambitious program of new laws for regulating sweatshops, closer supervision of utilities and insurance companies, new protections for women and children, and other initiatives. Boss Platt, for one, was furious and disgusted. "I want to get rid of the bastard," he complained. "I don't want him raising hell in my state any longer."[5]

Platt, a survivor of the Conkling Arthur fiasco, had a solution for the Roosevelt problem: the vice presidency. (Some people never learn.) McKinley was to be running for reelection in 1900, facing a rematch with Bryan, and Roosevelt on the ticket would substantially juice up the administration's staid image. Even better, the vice presidency would effectively muzzle Roosevelt. Hanna, for his part, was uneasy. "Don't any of you realize," he told the bosses who hatched the plan, "there's only one life between this madman and the White House?" Six months into his second term, McKinley became the third president in 36 years to be assassinated. Vice President Roosevelt had to be summoned from a mountain deep in the Adirondacks, where he was vacationing with his family. Hanna was beside himself. "Now look," he exclaimed, "that damned cowboy is President of the United States!"[6] Now, truly, the young dude—the youngest, in fact, in American history—would enter *the* arena.

He did so at the dawn of a new age: the Progressive Era. Progressivism is a complex phenomenon that has been the subject of debate for over a century, and so sprawling in its manifestations—playground reformers, antitrust lawyers, and tee-totaling

prohibitionists could and did plausibly claim the label—that
there were times when the concept seemed stretched to the point
of meaninglessness. What united them all were concerns about
the corrosive effects of corporate capitalism; attempts to rein in
such large private interests were the quintessential progressive
preoccupation. People like Henry Adams and TR's own father
were clearly direct forerunners of the progressives,[7] but the
movement discernibly picked up steam on the state and local levels in the 1890s, bubbling up into national politics by 1900.

Progressives had trouble gaining traction at the federal level,
however. The Interstate Commerce Act of 1887 was an important step toward establishing federal oversight of business prac-
tices, but the value of the law was mostly symbolic. Reformers
had placed great hopes on the Sherman Antitrust Act of 1890,
but the ironic effect of that law was its use by businesses to in-
hibit the power of unions. The 1895 Supreme Court case *U.S. v.
E.C. Knight* weakened the law further by affirming the right of a
holding company—a legal device created by huge companies to
play shell games with their capital—to acquire the stocks of its
competitors.

This anti-regulation counteroffensive was the backdrop of
one of the most audacious business mergers of all time: James J.
Hill's Great Northern Railroad, E. H. Harriman's Union Pacific
Railroad, and J. P. Morgan's Northern Pacific in November
1901. Harriman and Hill in particular had been fierce competitors, but had finally agreed to pool their resources into a vast
holding company, in the process creating a seventeen-state trust
that would stretch from Chicago to Seattle (and via Hill's foreign
lines, into China). This mega-company in the pivotal industry of
the age was to be known as the Northern Securities Company.
Mark Hanna rushed to buy stock.

Theodore Roosevelt had only been in office a few weeks
when the news of the Northern Securities Company hit the papers. Up until that point, his most important policy initiative involved the diplomatic spadework needed for a canal to bridge
the Atlantic and Pacific Oceans—Congress thought it should be
in Nicaragua, though TR favored Panama. In terms of public
opinion, the defining moment of his new presidency had been

his decision to invite Booker T. Washington—a Negro!—to dine at the White House in October of 1901. (This was the first time a black man had been anything but a waiter in the Executive Mansion; one newspaper described the invitation as "the most damnable outrage that has ever been perpetrated by a citizen of the United States").[8] In these opening weeks, TR had been buffing his first State of the Union address, taking the advice of those who urged him to tune down his rhetoric, even as he began meeting with his attorney general, Philander Chase Knox, about his legal options in taking on large corporations. That first major speech, delivered in December of 1901, paid ritualistic homage to titans of business, and the blessings of productivity, efficiency, and prosperity they engendered. But he also struck another note—a forceful new note that had never been heard coming from a president:

> Corporations engaged in interstate commerce should be regulated if they are found to exercise a license working to the public injury. It should be as much the aim of those who seek for social betterment to rid the business-world of crimes of cunning as to rid the entire body politic of crimes of violence. Great corporations exist only because they are created and safeguarded by our institutions; and it is therefore our right and our duty to see that they work in harmony with these institutions.[9]

But TR was not content with mere rhetoric. Forcefully and quickly, he formed a plan—a plan not to simply find a way around the *Knight* ruling, but to assault it directly. He moved stealthily, both to avoid panic on Wall Street and to achieve maximum political effect when he finally made his move. Like the young maverick in the New York Assembly, he still had a penchant for bold acts, but he had learned the arts of silence and surprise.

"What do you think of the Northern Securities Company?" he asked Mark Hanna, now a U.S. Senator from Ohio, during a breakfast meeting in Washington on February 18, 1902.[10] Hanna, distracted by an upcoming business trip to New York, described it as the best thing that had ever happened to the Northwest. On his way back home two days later, Hanna found himself on a train filled with chattering attorneys. When he ran into a former U.S. attorney general on the train, he asked what all the commotion was about. Hanna hadn't seen the morning papers? The president was suing the Northern Securities Company.

Stock exchanges around the world were reeling from the news. One of the few people who refused to panic was J. P. Morgan, who bought stocks steadily over the course of the morning. By the afternoon of February 20, prices had stabilized. The next day, Morgan, who had delegated a deputy to actually negotiate the Northern Securities deal, took six other representatives down to Washington. They had dinner with a group of associates, among them Republican U.S. Senator Chauncey Depew. Morgan himself also knew TR personally. At 10 P.M. a call came summoning his party to the White House. But nothing was resolved.

Morgan returned the next morning. What followed is a now legendary exchange between a maverick chief executive and the maverick financier who famously said, "I owe the public nothing." Why, Morgan asked, hadn't the Roosevelt administration simply asked him to resolve any potential illegalities in the Northern Securities Company's charter?

"That is just what we did not want to do," Roosevelt replied.

"If we have done anything wrong, send your man to my man and they can fix it up."

"That can't be done."

At this point, Attorney General Knox interjected, "We don't want to fix it up, we want to stop it."

"Are you going to attack my other interests, the Steel Trust and others?"

"Certainly not," TR replied, "unless we find out that in case that they have done something that we regard as wrong."

After Morgan had left, Roosevelt mused to Knox that their conversation had been "an illuminating illustration of the Wall Street point of view." Morgan, TR observed, viewed him as "a big rival operator." But the president was engaged in an entirely different line of business—a line of business that wasn't a business at all.[11]

The Northern Securities case would take two years to wind its way through the courts. It reached the end of the line in March of 1904, when it was finally taken up by the Supreme Court. Roosevelt was hoping for a decisive ruling in his favor, but was deeply uncertain about how the justices would rule, with the exception of his appointee, Oliver Wendell Holmes. It turned out that the Court did rule in the administration's favor, but by a slim 5–4 margin, with Holmes dissenting ("I could carve out of a banana a judge with more backbone than that," a disgusted Roosevelt complained of Holmes).[12] There was some fear that this was not going to be a decisive enough refutation of *Knight* and affirmation of the Sherman Act, but public opinion in the aftermath of the ruling suggested that Roosevelt was riding a wave of collective approval.

Roosevelt, in any case, had not been standing around and waiting for a decision from the Supreme Court on the Northern Securities Case. He launched dozens of antitrust cases, notably in the sugar and beef industries, and successfully took on another huge industrial colossus: John D. Rockefeller's Standard Oil. Such actions earned him the nickname of the "Trust-Buster," and if his hand-picked successor, William Howard Taft, actually launched more antitrust suits, it was Roosevelt who established the new government stance of monitoring and prosecuting corporate corruption.

This new vigor was not limited to lawsuits. In the early months of Roosevelt's presidency, a strike by anthracite coal workers in Pennsylvania and the industrial Midwest broke out, and as it continued through the summer and into the fall of 1902, labor unrest threatened the nation's coal supply for the coming winter. When state, local, or federal government had previously intervened in labor disputes, it had almost always done so by protecting the rights of owners to the point of firing on workers. Roosevelt, by contrast, became the first president to try and mediate an agreement. When the coal operators proved recalcitrant, Roosevelt made plans for the military to take over the coal mines and have the government run them. "What about the Constitution of the United States?" asked an incredulous James E. Watson, Republican leader in the House of Representatives. "What about seizing private property without due process of law?" An angry Roosevelt grabbed Watson by the shoulder and said, "The Constitution was made for the people and not the people for the Constitution." When negotiations got to the point of Roosevelt naming an independent commission, management refused to agree to have a labor representative present, though they did allow for the appointment of an eminent "sociologist." Fine, said TR—my sociologist will be the leader of the Railway Conductors Union.[13] The owners reluctantly acquiesced in the choice, and in the agreement that followed. "I was trying to save them from themselves," Roosevelt reflected a decade later, "and to avert, not only for their sakes, but for the sake of the country, the excesses which would have been indulged at their expense if they had persisted in their conduct."[14] He would not be the last Roosevelt to do so.

By this point, Roosevelt had been in office for a year—a debut that had been as forceful and impressive as any in American history. Only his hero, Abraham Lincoln, had presided over so many changes in so short a time, but Lincoln was more responding to events than implementing a vision. And Roosevelt was only getting started. The coming years would bring even more government initiatives: the Elkhorn and Hepburn Acts to empower the government further in interstate trade; the Pure Food and Drug Act, which established the government as the guardian of the health and welfare; a series of environmental initiatives that made the government the conservator of the nation's natural resources; and much more. He would win the Nobel Peace Prize for his role in brokering a treaty to end the Russo-Japanese War, oversee the completion of the Panama Canal (which involved wresting Panama away from Columbia), and send the American fleet on a goodwill tour around the world that made clear that, militarily, the United States had arrived.

His popularity continued to surge. Reelected handily in 1904, a third term would have been his for the asking if he had run again in 1908. But he had promised after his reelection that he would only serve two terms, and, ever restless, left the White House in 1909 and embarked on a celebrated African safari. Increasingly dissatisfied with the performance of the hand-picked

Taft, he edged back toward politics and declared his hat was "in the ring" in 1912. Amazingly, age had not mellowed TR: he moved farther to the left, declaring that "property shall be the servant and not the master," and advocating the adoption of an inheritance tax, government health insurance, choosing political candidates by direct primaries, and more powerful labor unions (subject to a more powerful federal government). When this platform was rejected at the Republican National Convention, he founded the Progressive, or "Bull Moose" Party. He out-polled Taft in the general election, but the split between them allowed the Democratic candidate, Woodrow Wilson—a man who had long admired Roosevelt—to win office. In 1912, all three of the major candidates considered themselves progressives, and the fourth, Eugene Debs, was a socialist. Idealism was a hot commodity.

There was a feverishness about Roosevelt now. He made a daunting expedition to Brazil ("I had to go. It was my last chance to be a boy"),[15] acquiring physical maladies that would dog him ever after. He complained that Wilson took too passive a position when the First World War broke out in 1914, demanding a harder line toward Germany. And when the United States entered the war in 1917, the 58-year-old TR begged Wilson for a battlefield commission, which Wilson refused to grant him. The death of two of his sons in the war finally knocked the wind out of Roosevelt. Now, at last showing signs of strain, he nevertheless made plans for a presidential campaign in 1920. He didn't make it, dying in January of 1919. Like so much else in his life, the end, when it came, was fast.

He's right up there on Mount Rushmore—with Washington, Jefferson (whom he detested), and Lincoln (whom he loved). At the time of the monument's dedication in 1927, there was some criticism among academics that not enough time had passed for an objective evaluation of Theodore Roosevelt, who had only been dead for eight years. But sculptor Gutzon Borglum, who had known TR, felt strongly that his friend belonged up there, and his judgment in this matter is largely considered correct. A century after his presidency, Roosevelt is still among the most admired of American presidents, regarded as a true giant among—and by—the dozens who have held the post.

Up close, however, he becomes less a gigantic character than a cartoon character. His characteristic declamations of "Dee-lighted!" and "Bully!"; the breathless accounts of big-game hunts that stretch across Africa and the Americas; the slogans about the strenuous life and speaking softly while carrying a big stick; even the fad of the Teddy Bear that he inspired—it's like he's some nostalgia act whose greatest hits get sliced, diced, and recombined for cable television documentaries and even advertisements (as his recent biographer, Kathleen Dalton, has noted, TR's name has been used to promote everything from computer diskettes to investment firms).[16] In an age that was decisively black and white, there remains, even now, something insistently colorful about him. The vitality of the big new world seemed to surge through him like a neon current.

It's in the middle distance, viewing Roosevelt in the context of the presidency generally, that he comes into the sharpest focus. The United States had had strong presidents before, but TR changed the nature of the presidency itself, establishing its function as a "bully pulpit" in framing national debates (he was the first president to have regular press conferences, albeit in a barber's chair) and making it as much an originator of legislation as a conduit for it. Indeed, it was as an actor—i.e., one who executes actions, as well as in the sense of someone who embodies a role—that Roosevelt permanently changed our default setting for the presidency, from an office where one presides to one where one assumes, in the broadest sense of that verb, the qualities of leadership.

It is—the present tense seems singularly apropos—not always easy to like Theodore Roosevelt. But it is difficult not to admire him. In the utter impatience with which he acted to change his country for the sake of continuity to its ideals, he moved millions—some in directions where they would rather not go, but where it was best they did. A hundred years later, he moves us still.

*(previous page)* FRANKLY DISINGENUOUS: President Roosevelt in the first year of his administration, December 1933. An enormously magnetic personality, Roosevelt was also notorious for his lack of transparency in governing the nation. In the case of the Supreme Court, this approach caught up with him. Yet his political skills proved essential in preparing the nation for the challenge of the Second World War. (Presidential Portraits, Library of Congress)

CHAPTER SIX

# F.D.R. COURTS DISASTER

*In which we see a handicapped man*
*learn he must not be a bully*
*if he wants to save the world from despotism*

In early 1937, as he began the second term of his presidency, Franklin Delano Roosevelt overreached in a way that some people at the time believed resembled the power grabs of Hitler and Mussolini. This was possible in large measure because he was at the zenith of his popularity. Roosevelt had been reelected in 1936 by a crushing margin, taking 46 out of 48 states (only rock-ribbed Republican Maine and Vermont went for his opponent, Kansas governor, and virtual afterthought, Alf Landon). He won 61 percent of the popular vote to Landon's 37 percent and his electoral college tally was a lopsided 523 to 8. Rarely have an American president's policies been so resoundingly vindicated by the electorate.

Of course, these were unusual times. Roosevelt came to office in 1933 in the depths of the Great Depression, offering his fellow Americans a "New Deal." They weren't altogether sure what this meant, because Roosevelt wasn't, either—to a great extent, he made his presidency up as he went along, beginning with a torrent of improvised legislative initiatives that were passed by Congress virtually without resistance. The twin pillars of the New Deal were the National Industrial Recovery Act (NIRA) and the Agricultural Adjustment Act (AAA), which codified a set of reforms for the two largest sectors of the American economy upon their passage in 1933. Roosevelt followed with a series of so-called Alphabet Agencies—FERA, CCC, PWA, etc.[1]—that primed the economy with government spending, and, perhaps more importantly, engendered confidence among the American people that a committed leader was attacking their problems in a serious way. When a series of more radical voices threatened to make the Roosevelt administration appear timid, the president responded with the so-called Second New Deal of 1935, which resulted in the creation of the Social Security System and the passage of the National Labor Relations (or Wagner) Act, which guaranteed labor unions the right to engage in collective bargaining. This maneuver protected Roosevelt's flank—and protected American capitalism from critics who wanted to shackle it even more than Roosevelt did. Such political instincts, perhaps even more than the content of the programs themselves, paved the way for FDR to cruise toward reelection in 1936. He was now the towering colossus of American politics.

Which is not to say he lacked opponents, even avowed enemies. Though some businessmen were impressed and encouraged by Roosevelt's reinvigoration of the American economy, many others resented the higher taxes, greater regulation, and concentrated government power the New Deal imposed. Roosevelt himself had found it politically expedient to excoriate "economic royalists," and in a famous campaign speech at Madison Square Garden in October of 1936 had declared, "They are unanimous in their hatred of me—and I welcome their hatred."[2] Though he was careful to leave these haters unnamed (in contrast to some other world leaders of the time, Roosevelt avoided demonizing specific people or groups), there is little doubt of their existence. One group, the Liberty League, was essentially an anti-Roosevelt organization that couched its opposition in terms of tradition and patriotism.

Roosevelt believed that his most formidable opponent was not the U.S. business community, but the U.S. Supreme court.

Somewhat unusually, there had not been a single opening on the court during his first term, which was dominated by septuagenarians from Republican administrations (six of the nine justices were over seventy years old). Again and again, the court had struck down New Deal initiatives in a series of 5–4 decisions, notably the NIRA and key provisions of the AAA. In the coming months, the justices would be weighing the constitutionality of the Social Security and National Labor Relations Acts. The court had not been able to completely shut down the New Deal, many of whose initiatives were only temporary anyway. But Roosevelt was determined to remove this deeply annoying obstacle in his path—and resorted to unorthodox means to achieve that goal.

He set about the task of subverting the judiciary in his typical way: by delegating the same job to different people, unbeknownst to each other, and seeing what bubbled up. One proposal that emerged was for a bill whereby Supreme Court invalidations of a federal or state law could be overturned by a two-thirds majority in Congress, or a simple majority after an intervening election. This was unlikely to pass in anything like an expedient manner. Another proposal, which came from FDR's attorney general, Homer Cummings, was more audacious. Part of what made it so was its inspiration, which came from Associate Court Justice James C. McReynolds, who, as attorney general himself in 1913, had proposed that any federal judge over seventy years old would have another judge appointed by the president and hold precedent over the older one. McReynolds exempted Supreme Court justices from his unsuccessful proposal. But why, Cummings asked, stop there? "The answer to a maiden's prayer!" FDR reputedly said when he heard the proposal.[3]

Roosevelt unveiled his plan to Congress in February of 1937 as an administrative reform measure. The court's docket, he explained, was very full, and the presence of so many senior citizens running it inevitably slowed the wheels of justice. That's why he proposed the appointment of a new justice for every judge over seventy, up to a maximum of 15. Since the number of justices had varied throughout American history, from six in 1789 to the current nine, adding up to a half-dozen more was no big deal. The nation could have the good government it deserved.

Roosevelt fooled nobody. He didn't care. Nor did he care when Chief Justice Charles Evans Hughes provided statistical evidence of the court's efficiency. Nor did he care that many members of his own party were appalled by the proposal. He didn't even care when the court, whether responding to the furor or not, made a series of decisions in Roosevelt's favor ("a switch in time saves nine," joked an assistant to presidential adviser Felix Frankfurter, who would himself be appointed to sit on the high court by FDR). Week after week, month after month, Roosevelt insisted on his bill, that very insistence draining his credibility and emboldening his opponents. Finally, in July of 1937, his vice president, John Nance Garner, told him, "If you want it with the bark off, you're licked, Cap'n. You haven't got the votes." Garner, a presidential hopeful in 1940, was not among those who grieved at the prospect of a presidential embarrassment. Roosevelt ordered him to do what he could to save face for the administration, which resulted in a new law with minor adjustments to judicial procedure.[4]

It was the biggest defeat of Roosevelt's presidency. In a way, it didn't matter—the circumstances that prompted the court-packing scheme suddenly dissipated in mid-1937. Not only did the court, perhaps belatedly responding to electoral returns, begin ruling Roosevelt's way (notably in decisions upholding the Social Security and National Labor Relations Acts), but a quick wave of retirements allowed FDR to finally mold the court in his own image. After having no appointments in his first term, Roosevelt got to make five in the first three years of his second. This gave the Supreme Court a liberal tilt that would remain in place for the next half-century.

But if FDR had unexpectedly won the battle, it was far less clear that he had won the war. The critics who emerged in the court-packing fight did not scatter to the winds in its aftermath. In particular, Southern Democrats who had never been happy with the urban tilt of their party teamed up with Republicans to limit further New Deal initiatives. Moreover, one did not have to be a pampered millionaire or a segregationist reactionary to wonder if this man—any man—should have the power Roosevelt did. Other wildly popular leaders had used their mandate to centralize their authority in deeply alarming ways. It was not irrational to think it could happen here.

Indeed, it was not irrational to think it *was* happening here. The Roosevelt administration was not a one-man show, and was comprised of talented and idealistic people, stretching from his Columbia University–based "Brain Trust" to the informal, but invaluable, contributions of FDR's wife, Eleanor. But Roosevelt was always in charge, and he was no more of a saint in his public life than he was in his private life.[5] To many of his contemporaries, FDR was an enigmatic figure, and in an important sense the better you got to know him the better you knew you never really would. His blinding charm rarely invited intimacy, and he took pride in his ability to dissemble. Roosevelt could also be vindictive, in ways that ranged from wickedly mischievous (like appointing Irishman Joseph P. Kennedy, a fascist sympathizer with dubious credentials, as U.S. ambassador to Britain) to alarmingly subversive (like using the Internal Revenue Service to harass enemies, among them former treasury secretary Andrew Mellon). He became less prone to claim credit for things he didn't do as his stature grew, but was never one to reflect upon, never mind admit, mistakes.

In any event, the national situation appeared to be spiraling out of anyone's control by the late 1930s. The economic downturn of 1937–38 suggested that the Rooseveltian magic had run its course. And the international scene became progressively darker by decade's end. When making the unprecedented decision to run for a third term in 1940, a key premise of the Roosevelt campaign was a pledge that no American boys would be sent overseas. Amid the political, social, and cultural divisions that wracked American society, there was basic consensus on that point. Roosevelt would tamper with it at his peril.

In the lifetimes of most of us, the United States has been deeply engaged in the affairs of the world. We have intervened in some wars (Korea, 1950), started others (Iraq, 2003), and participated extensively in global trade. Even after quagmires like Vietnam, few have seriously questioned the legitimacy, even the necessity, for U.S. immersion in world affairs, even if there has often been disagreement about the length or legitimacy of a specific intervention.

The pervasiveness of U.S. engagement in our time has led many of us to forget that for most of American history, isolation, not intervention, has been the basis of U.S. foreign policy. As he departed from the presidency, George Washington warned his fellow Americans against "entangling alliances" that would compromise their independence. Thomas Jefferson decided he would rather refuse to trade with England and France than be forced to choose between them. The famous Monroe Doctrine, written by John Quincy Adams, warned European powers that further colonial expansion in the western hemisphere would be viewed as an unfriendly act, and Theodore Roosevelt added a corollary in 1904 saying that the United States would intervene in Latin American nations before allowing European powers to get involved. Even the highly successful Mexican and Spanish-American Wars had large peace movements, whose antiwar opposition mingled humanitarian and racist motives.

The greatest exception to the American rule of isolation was the First World War. Here, unmistakably, was a decisive intervention: the United States threw its full weight into that war in 1917, and that weight made all the difference. It's important to note, however, that American involvement came notably late; the war began in 1914 with virtually universal agreement among Americans that the country should stay out of it, and Woodrow Wilson (who personally had a distinctly pro-Allied view of the struggle) won reelection in 1916 with a campaign slogan that "He Kept Us Out of War." Perhaps even more important, the aftermath of American involvement in the war was marked by a widespread sense of disenchantment, one that manifest itself in ways that ranged from U.S. refusal to participate in the League of Nations, common accusations that the war was really fought for the benefit of international arms merchants, and a modernist cultural movement (embodied by figures like Gertrude Stein and Earnest Hemingway) that viewed idealism as a fool's game and nationalism as a form of mass-brainwashing.

Roosevelt came into office well aware of this history, in part because to a great extent he had lived it. For all their differences, Wilson and Theodore Roosevelt ("Uncle Ted" to FDR, who was in fact his fifth cousin and married the niece TR considered a virtual daughter) were finally decisive internationalists, and FDR himself fully shared their sentiments. As assistant secretary of the Navy, he wriggled under the authority of his isolationist boss, Josephus Daniels, continuing to hold internationalist views as long as it was practical to do so. But FDR had also seen Wilson overplay his hand in the aftermath of the First World War, demanding U.S. involvement in the League of Nations on Wilsonian terms and getting nothing, and he was well aware of the strength of isolationist sentiment when he came into office. Since his first priority was in any case dealing with the Great Depression, he deferred arguing with men who in domestic affairs could be important allies.

This sense of political priorities is essential to the success of any politician, and FDR was an absolute master of gauging them realistically. So, for example, he signed the Neutrality Act of 1935, which prohibited American citizens from selling arms to belligerents in international war (it was generated in response to Italy's invasion of Abysinnia), even though he had reservations about it. He went along with an even stronger law in 1937, which added civil wars to the Neutrality Act's purview (this in response to the outbreak of the Spanish Civil War, which pitted fascists against socialists and communists). In these and other cases, the Neutrality Acts of the 1930s gave the president discretion to invoke them by finding that a state of war existed in a particular instance. This provided a loophole that Roosevelt could potentially exploit at some point.

It is a coincidence of history that Roosevelt's presidency was almost exactly concurrent with the rule of Adolf Hitler—they came to office and died within weeks of each other. For most of the 1930s, Americans regarded Hitler's rise to power as a regrettable, but largely irrelevant, development, much in the way they regarded imperial Japan's aggression against China. Roosevelt, by contrast, recognized these powers for the globally destabilizing forces they were, and resolved to challenge them when the time was right.

By about 1937, that time had arrived. As with the court-packing scheme, FDR had embarked on a course decisively at odds with public opinion. He knew this, but was determined to proceed anyway. There were, however, two decisive differences. The first is that Roosevelt's motivation in court-packing was primarily political and tactical—he wanted to get his way—whereas in the case of the looming international scene his motivation was about preparing Americans for things no one wanted but that might nevertheless be inevitable. The second, and perhaps more important distinction is the manner he went about securing the objectives in question. In the case of court-packing, FDR was bull-headed and tone deaf. In the case of swaying public opinion toward international fascism, he was both careful and deft.

In a way, Roosevelt's problem with American isolationism in the 1930s and '40s was a little like Abraham Lincoln's problem with slavery in the 1850s and '60s. Though isolationists and slaveholders had their defenders, some of whom invoked natural law, most people agreed that the behavior of Germany, Italy, and Japan, like the behavior of slaveholders, was morally wrong, and that someone ought to do something about them at some point. But not us. Not now. Both Lincoln and Roosevelt professed respect for these views, and made active steps to affirm them. Lincoln, for example, countermanded the orders of generals who freed slaves early in the Civil War, while FDR stretched, but finally observed, limits on the number of Jewish refugees he allowed into the United States—measures for which both men received criticism then and subsequently. But there was a lingering, and ultimately founded, suspicion about both men that they intended to lead the country in a different direction than popular opinion was dictating.

In contrast to the court-packing scheme, Roosevelt went about reshaping conventional wisdom in an exquisitely calibrated way. The starting point was his so-called Quarantine the Aggressors speech of October of 1937, which he delivered in Chicago, the heart of the isolationist Midwest. In the months before the speech, the Spanish Civil War was raging, Japan had invaded Nanking, and Hitler had occupied the neutral zone between Germany and France. Roosevelt noted that Americans were fortunate that "the circumstances of the moment permit us to put our money into bridges and boulevards, dams and reforestation, the conservation of our soil and many other kinds of useful works rather than into huge standing armies and vast supplies of implements of war."[6] (The key words of that sentence, almost lost among the laundry list of public works, is "the circumstances of the moment.") He ended the speech with an extended metaphor of aggression as a disease that must be contained—a vague suggestion that nevertheless generated substantial discussion, as FDR intended—and concluded with a ritual affirmation of the need for peace.

Roosevelt coupled his ambiguous rhetoric with less ambiguous actions. So, for example, while he signed and professed to honor the Neutrality Act of 1937, he asserted (with somewhat dubious logic) that the situation China faced with Japan was not in fact a state of war, and thus the act's provisions did not apply, thus allowing support for China. In 1939, as World War II formally got underway, the administration persuaded Congress to roll back the Neutrality Act, though there was one new provision banning American shipping from war zones, along with another one known as "cash and carry," requiring trading partners to pay in advance for, and haul away, war materiel. Since only Britain and France were in this position by that point, the onerous new law nevertheless had a pro-Allied tilt.

By 1940, when he made the decision to pursue a third term, Roosevelt's arguments had taken another step. Now, he argued, the only way to keep the United States out of the war was to reject isolationism, to aid the Allies as much as possible, so their success would prevent the United States from having to get involved. This approach, "preparedness," had the added advantage of stimulating the economy, since the increased defense spending that Roosevelt sought and received resulted in thousands of new jobs and a permanent end to the Great Depression. The argument was successful and Roosevelt was again reelected, albeit by a smaller margin than the first two times.

Even after his reelection, however—even after Paris had fallen to the Nazis, Britain was being bombed, and most of East Asia was under Japanese control—interventionism continued to be the dominant national mood. To many, the war still seemed oceans away; most people had not considered, as FDR had, what might happen if Nazism spread to dictatorship-susceptible Latin America, or if the British Navy fell under German control. Roosevelt, still angling for better ways to help Britain, devised what became known as the "Lend-Lease Act," a politically and militarily creative piece of statecraft. Lend-Lease would allow him to give the British armaments he deemed necessary for the defense of the United States, in exchange for assets that ranged from financial credits to military bases that Britain would turn over to the United States. In a famous December 1940 press conference, he compared Lend-Lease to handing your garden hose to a neighbor whose house was on fire. "I don't say to him, 'Neighbor, my garden hose cost me $15; you have got to pay me $15 for it.' What is the transaction that goes on? I don't want $15—I want my garden hose back when the fire is over.'" And if, as is possible, the hose gets "smashed up—holes in it," the neighbor will simply buy him a new hose later.[7] This combination of homespun metaphor and political muscle got FDR the law he wanted in March of 1941. When Hitler turned on his erstwhile ally, the Soviet Union, by invading Russia in June that year, Lend-Lease was extended to the Soviets as well, providing an invaluable lifeline for an alliance that was on the ropes.

Still the United States remained outside the ring. Roosevelt realized it would remain there unless it was actively provoked by one of the belligerents, but perhaps that would not take too much longer. The Japanese were boxed in by a strategic dilemma. The resource-poor empire depended on economic expansion for growth, and particularly needed petroleum to fuel that expansion. Well into the 1930s, its principal supplier was the United States, but further aggression would lead the United States to cut off its supply.[8] On the other hand, conquering the vast Dutch oil fields of the East Indies would solve the fuel problem but antagonize the United States. Concluding that there was no way around it, Japanese imperialists laid their plans for the attack on Pearl Harbor. There is no real evidence to the longstanding rumor that Roosevelt knew that particular attack was coming (if nothing else, it's unlikely a Navy man would willingly consent to the destruction of a third of his battle fleet), but it is nevertheless clear that he did expect—and, yes, hope for—an attack that would free him from the burden of isolationism and empower him to act decisively. Hitler also played into FDR's hands by declaring war the next day on the United States, something his treaty with the Japanese did not require him to do unless the U.S. had been the aggressor, but something he had long wanted to do and something that, on the cusp of his seemingly inevitable success against the Soviets, made a manic kind of sense.

In an important sense, Roosevelt's role in the Second World War was a replay, on a larger scale, of his role in the Great Depression: to convey a sense of competence and confidence to the United States and its allies. He did this—along with some of his usual double-dealing—with marvelous assurance. It had appeared that Roosevelt was at the zenith of his power in 1937. Instead, he reached that zenith during the Second World War, when his powers, immense as they were, were wielded with a genuinely becoming modesty when compared with monsters like Hitler or Stalin (and even with FDR's great ally, the comparably heroic, but much more overtly egomaniacal, Winston Churchill). Roosevelt was guilty of excesses, notably in consenting to the massive relocation of Japanese citizens in California (a fate which escaped the much more numerous Japanese of Hawaii, and a crime which was opposed by even the notorious FBI chief J. Edgar Hoover), but even they were mild compared to those of his opponents, and more a matter of a failure to restrain racist excesses than a policy he initiated. As Jews and African Americans knew, Roosevelt was a mortal man, not a divine angel.

Supervising the American war effort was a daunting task even for a healthy person, which, as the war proceeded, Roosevelt increasingly ceased to be. Reelected to a fourth term in 1944, the American public was largely unaware that he was by this point ailing, even faltering. There have been longstanding complaints that his physical weakness led him astray at Yalta in 1945, where he supposedly gave away the store to Stalin, though it's hard to see how Roosevelt had much choice—or how, for better or worse, his stance toward Stalin (what might be termed indulgent skepticism), had ever been much different. Roosevelt was only in the second month of his fourth term when, during a vacation stop at Warm Springs on his way to the founding of the United Nations in San Francisco, he died of a cerebral hemorrhage. He was 63 years old.

Historians today are virtually unanimous that an imprecise but unmistakable psychological power lay at the heart of Roosevelt's success as president. Indeed, some go so far to say that as a matter of policy, the New Deal was, in fact, a failure, one whose empirical shortcomings were already apparent by the late thirties as the nation's economic performance, which had recovered so impressively by mid-decade, began to decline precipitously. These assertions are true as far as they go. But they ultimately mattered less than FDR's ability to both reassure and move public opinion in ways that bought him time and mobilized collective action. Had Roosevelt behaved the way he had with the court-packing, he might well have alienated the public, with a result something like that described by Philip Roth in his 2004 novel *The Plot Against America*, in which the proto-fascist aviator/celebrity Charles Lindbergh becomes president.

Indeed, it's important to remember that Roosevelt was not infallible in wielding his political skills. The court-packing scheme demonstrated that his will sometimes got the better of him, and that his exercise of power could indeed take on the overtones of the very forces in Depression-era life he was most committed to opposing, particularly in his centralization of political power. But even when such lapses were exposed and defeated, there was sufficient strength and restraint for him to meet the greatest challenge of twentieth-century life. Winston Churchill provided much of the inspiration, and Josef Stalin provided the blood and guts that proved crucial in overcoming that challenge. But it was a massive industrial engine of aircraft carriers and bullets—and chocolate bars, and panty hose, and paperback books with stirring covers— that ultimately steamrollered the Axis powers. Roosevelt maneuvered this awesome force into position through the force of his imperfect, but finally decisive, powers of persuasion.

A lifetime later, a bunch of empires have come and gone, and Pax Americana remains, however tentatively, in place. Some social welfare protections of the New Deal have been nibbled away at and perhaps have outlived their usefulness, but they, too, remain largely in place, despite the determined attempts of some presidents, among them Ronald Reagan and George W. Bush, to dismantle them. In important respects, this is still Roosevelt's world. We just live in it. In the half-life of its afterglow, we're damned lucky.

*(previous page)* LIFE OF THE PARTY: Lyndon Johnson, White House portrait, 1964. Neither Johnson's writings nor his television appearances capture the gigantic force of his will, talent, and humor, which routinely overwhelmed ally and opponent alike. Over the course of his long career, he wielded that power selfishly and altruistically with often stunning effectiveness. (Presidential Portraits, Library of Congress)

## CHAPTER SEVEN

# "LANDSLIDE LYNDON" TAKES A POSITION

*In which we see an amoral opportunist commit an act of courage*

The key to avoiding a recount, Abe Fortas told the collection of lawyers in the big conference room, will be to find a federal judge to whom we can make an appeal that we *know* will be refused.[1] When we lose, it will mean the case against us will go forward. But it also means we can appeal again—via an emergency ruling by a Supreme Court justice I know will overturn it. This judge will deny that the feds have any jurisdiction in what we're claiming is a state matter, not a civil rights case. Once states' rights get affirmed, the road will be clear for Lyndon Baines Johnson to become the next senator from the great state of Texas.

Not an orthodox political strategy to be sure, especially coming from a future justice of the Supreme Court.[2] But this was a desperate situation. All through that scorching hot summer of 1948, Congressman Johnson had been scouring the Texas countryside trawling for votes in his quixotic quest for a U.S. Senate seat. His principal opponent for the Democratic nomination—in an essentially one-party state where the primary was the only election that mattered—was Governor Coke Stevenson. Stevenson was a legendary figure in Texas politics, the archetypal Western rancher beloved for his laconic honesty and integrity. Johnson had begun the race impossibly behind, but through a Herculean effort that involved new campaign techniques like paid radio advertisements and transportation by private helicopter, as well as old-fashioned ones like huge cash payments in envelopes from shadowy donors, he had whittled down Stevenson's lead (as measured by the novel approach of daily polling). He was still behind on primary day, but captured enough of the vote to finish second in the three-man contest and force a runoff. In the next leg of the contest, he continued his relentless barrage of negative campaigning: His opponent was portrayed as a communist stooge, a tool of organized labor, and, simultaneously, a puppet of large commercial interests. Stevenson, a politician of the old school, was bewildered by this blizzard of invective, much of it verifiably false, but trusted voters to see through it. His faith appeared justified: On Election Day, the Johnson storm did not blow him down.

And so Johnson was forced to resort to a more traditional technique of Texas politics: fraud. This was the device that had blasted Johnson's previous bid for the Senate in 1941, when he had taken on another popular governor, W. L. "Pappy" O'Daniel. Johnson had probably won that race, but at the last moment liquor interests in Texas, concerned that O'Daniel, a teetotaler, would bar drinking from the soldiers now flooding into the state's army and naval bases, decided it would be better to kick him upstairs to Washington. An overconfident Johnson had already reported his vote totals in the precincts where he was strongest, which made it easy for "late" reporting of previously uncounted "votes" for O'Daniel from other districts to edge him out.

Now, determined not to make such mistakes again, Johnson battened down his own hatches and set up an operation in Mexican-dominated South Texas, where his minions paid poll taxes and harvested votes from precincts whose results trickled in days later, results that went in Johnson's favor by absurd (like 90 percent plus margins). Johnson would later boast of his machinations in a joke he would tell of a little Mexican boy who was alternatively named Manuel or Jesus, who sat on a corner in a border town, crying. When a friend came up and asked what the trouble was, the boy would say, "My father was in town last Saturday, and he did not come to see me."

"But Manuel, your father has been dead for ten years," the story would go.

Manuel sobbed louder. "Sí, he has been dead for ten years. But he came to town last Saturday to vote for Lyndon Johnson, and he did not come to see me!"[3]

But in the summer of 1948, when the "final" count went to Johnson by "87" votes, this was no laughing matter. Certainly it wasn't for Stevenson, who, along with a trusted Texas Ranger, went South to investigate, like two characters in a Clint Eastwood movie. They found all kinds of evidence of foul play, like the testimony of people whose votes were recorded but who never went to the polls. They also found a smoking gun: a box of votes from a precinct that had clearly been tampered with (among other indicators, the perpetrators hadn't even bothered to use the same color ink when altering the original voting lists). A legal tug of war followed in a series of rulings between Stevenson and Johnson. Stevenson's position was consistent: He wanted the truth to be known. Johnson's position was not: He alternately argued that there was no fraud, that Stevenson had committed fraud, too, that fraud had always been part of elections, that there was no legal recourse for it in any case.

There was also a national dimension to the context. Nineteen-forty-eight was a presidential election year, and Harry S. Truman was seeking reelection in a very tough fight. Southern conservatives, angered by Truman's stand on civil rights—he had desegregated the armed forces the previous year by executive order—had bolted the Democrats to form a "States Rights Party" in four Southern states. Behind in the polls, Truman was desperate for Texas to remain in the fold. He had his differences with Johnson—for good reason, Truman suspected LBJ played both sides of factional fences—but he had more confidence in Johnson than in the unambiguously conservative Stevenson. Johnson narrowly carried the day with the Texas Democratic Party's State Executive Committee, which certified him as the nominee.

Stevenson wasn't through yet, however. He convinced a federal judge to hear the case to decide whether the national government had jurisdiction to intervene in the election. A new round of legal wrangling followed, during which the evidence was retrieved and edged closer to being opened. Witnesses suddenly developed faulty memories on the stand, and relevant documents simply disappeared. The judge, exasperated, tried to cut the knot with a disarmingly simple offer: Why not just run the election over, "and let the people of Texas decide the winner?"

Sounds good to me, Stevenson said on the spot.

"No comment," said Johnson as he made his way out of the courtroom for a noon recess.[4]

Johnson's attorneys urged him to accept the proposal. He categorically refused. He had given up a safe seat in the Congress to enter this race, and the deadline to reapply had passed. He had poured his blood and guts into the race (literally: he had been hospitalized with a dreadful kidney stone early in the campaign, and stayed in the race by sheer force of will), and he was going for broke. Besides, it was by no means clear that he could win a rerun, fairly or otherwise.

The hearing resumed, and it went poorly for Johnson, as attendees heard testimony from supposed voters who in reality had been hundreds of miles away from the polls on Election Day. This is a civil rights case, the judge ruled, and thus a federal matter. He issued an injunction barring Johnson's name from appearing on the ballot in the coming general election pending further investigation—by which point it might be too late for him to even be listed as an option for voters to choose. Unless something happened quickly, Johnson's quest would be over. His lawyers were stumped.

Enter Abe Fortas. Johnson's old friend, who he had first met as a fellow New Dealer during Johnson's days as a wheeling-dealing staff member for playboy congressman Richard Kleberg, had become a powerful Washington attorney. By sheer coincidence, he was in Dallas when Johnson sought him out. Fortas came to Fort Worth, where Johnson was huddling with his attorneys, and evaluated the situation.

There was no way to win the case on the merits, Fortas pointed out, because even if Johnson got a ruling he wanted, Stevenson would challenge it, forcing delays beyond Election Day, with the likely result of a blank Democratic ballot—in which case a Republican might actually win the November election. What they needed, he argued, was to challenge whether the federal judge had jurisdiction. If they made the case and lost, Fortas could then appeal to the U.S. Supreme Court. The justice who would make an emergency ruling on cases in this district was Hugo Black, and Fortas was confident that Black would rule that the federal court would not have jurisdiction in what he would regard as a state matter. (Just what the basis of this confidence was has never been completely established.)

The next day, one of Johnson's attorneys flew to New Orleans to file an appeal with a judge who had once ruled that no injunction could be overturned without a concurrence of three judges. Not surprisingly, he rejected the case (but unexpectedly took five agonizing hours to do so). The federal case went forward, and various boxes were being sorted and opened at the very moment word came from Justice Black: The feds had no jurisdiction, and the case was to be suspended immediately. Johnson appeared on the ballot, easily defeated his Republican opponent, and took his seat in the U.S. Senate—all thanks to the classic states' rights position that had been a part of Southern politics going back to the time of Thomas Jefferson.

"Landslide Lyndon," they called him. Even Johnson himself used the nickname. He could afford to take a joke; after all, he had gotten what he wanted—power. The question, for which he had no obvious reply, was what he planned to do with it.

Lyndon Johnson had an extraordinary capacity for exploiting people. It was manifest early in his life in multiple ways, whether in the chores he got his younger brother to do for him or his ability to wheedle free housing and good campus jobs out of the president of San Marcos Teachers College, the first of many men, most importantly House Speaker Sam Rayburn, to adopt

Johnson as his protégé. The focus of his activities was often triv-
ial, like student elections, but Johnson was able to invest them
with a shared significance and achieve the desired results by applying his considerable intelligence. This didn't make him particularly well-liked—indeed, in some quarters, it made him
cordially hated—but Johnson was willing and able to find con-
federates to do his bidding and became sufficiently influential so
that even those who didn't like him thought twice about saying
so, never mind defying him. At the core of this talent lay a profound psychological ability of taking another person's measure
and inhabiting it with unusual intensity and predictive power.
This allowed him to tap the hopes and fears of mentor and minion alike with remorseless clarity. So it was that he could charm
a target mercilessly: Survivors of the so-called Johnson Treatment—in which he would pull your lapel, literally get in your
face, wheedle, promise, threaten, and flatter you, seemingly all
at once—were often awed by the experience.

Johnson also had an extraordinary capacity for empathy,
though this quality was generally held in check (unless, of course, it
could be deployed for some practical purpose). Early in his career,
as a newly elected congressman in the late 1930s, he tirelessly and
brilliantly manipulated New Deal machinery to bring rural electri-
fication to West Texas, literally transforming the lives of his isolated rural constituents. His years in the House of Representatives
were typically focused on his own advancement—Johnson was
never one to introduce, or even try to pass, legislation—though he
was capable of the impulsive gesture, as when he procured a burial
at Arlington National Cemetery for a Mexican American con-
stituent who had died in the line of duty in World War II, but had
been denied one in his hometown. (He kept his role as quiet as
possible when racists in his district complained.)

As with the young Abraham Lincoln, race relations were a
distraction to LBJ—albeit a distraction that had a way of seeming
to surface everywhere you turned. Johnson was a Texan, which is
to say he was a (particular kind of) Southerner, which is to say he
inherited a set of racial attitudes that he carried with him
throughout his life. Actually, the Texas Hill Country of his origins—his people had been there for generations, and his father

had represented the region in the state legislature before the collapse of his fortunes after the First World War—had relatively few African Americans. While Johnson tended to exaggerate his degree of racial enlightenment, he probably was less racist than many of his congressional colleagues, though he tended to adjust his pitch—whether, for example, he used the term "negro," or "nigra" or "nigger"—depending on with whom he was talking and what he hoped to gain. Though many people, pro- and con, cared about them deeply, Johnson tended to think about things like segregation, voting rights, and racial equality at best as means to an end.

Because he spent most of his career as part of a Southern delegation, mere political survival generally dictated that Johnson hew to a segregationist party line. The Democrats had been solid in the South for a century following the Civil War, and those politicians who were not frank about their racism—plenty were—tended to justify their policies in terms of states' rights. This was the approach of the courtly and powerful Richard Russell of Georgia, Johnson's mentor and patron in the Senate.

Southern cohesion and political skill had allowed the region to dominate the Senate, effectively making it the most powerful bulwark against Civil Rights in the federal government. Yet as Russell realized, the South would never finish the process of reintegration into the body politic as long as segregation was the cornerstone of Southern life. Russell had seen his own hopes for the presidency founder on this conundrum. That's why he cut Johnson slack when LBJ tried to gain liberal approval and trust in passing the Civil Rights Act of 1957, a law ridiculously weak in promoting voter registration (it had been stripped of its anti-segregation provisions, and allowed all-white juries to try violators). The Civil Rights movement would have never gotten off the ground if it had depended on white men in Washington—democratic in the most profound sense, the movement was a grassroots enterprise led by citizens, many of them women, who acted with a profound faith in the power of the people to compel change. But Johnson's phone calls, horse trading and arm twisting were crucial to the symbolically significant law, the first Civil Rights statute to clear Congress in 82 years.

He hoped this accomplishment would win over liberal skeptics and yield him the Democratic nomination for president in
1960. But Johnson, the ultimate insider who always came across
as hopelessly stiff on the newly dominant medium of television,
didn't have a chance against handsome Jack Kennedy—an empty
suit as a senator from Massachusetts, but simply smashing as a
presidential candidate.[5] In the eyes of Southern conservatives,
Kennedy lacked gravitas and trustworthiness. And so it was that
JFK turned to LBJ to be his running mate. Calculating that it was
the right move but dreading it, Johnson campaigned energeti-
cally for Kennedy, and probably provided him with a critical
margin of victory in Johnson's native Texas. Upon relinquishing
his position as majority leader of the Senate, Johnson was
promptly marginalized by Kennedy in ways that fed every inse-
curity of a boy from the sticks, however talented, in the shadow
of an Eastern city-slicker.

Nowhere was this more apparent than in Civil Rights matters. Kennedy and his attorney general brother, Robert, strug-
gled to keep abreast of (and contain) lunch-counter sit-ins,
Freedom Rides, and voter registration drives, and parried with
wily segregationists like Governor George Wallace of Alabama.
Meanwhile, Johnson, who could have really been helpful to the
administration, moped his way through Latin American funer-
als and even paid a visit to the remote nation of Vietnam, far
from the nation's collective radar in the Camelot days of the
early sixties.

And then, suddenly, Kennedy was dead. Deeply shaken by
the way he had achieved his lifelong dream, Johnson recognized
that he had an opportunity when he assumed office—an opportunity to do well by doing good. Sensing the prevailing political
winds, he made race relations the vehicle by which he would
make his mark. "No memorial oration or eulogy could more elo-
quently honor President Kennedy's memory than the earliest
possible passage of the civil rights bill for which he fought so
long," he told a joint session of Congress on November 27, 1963,
four days after the assassination. Less than a week later, he had
Martin Luther King, Jr. to the White House for the first of a series of visits, and King saw in Johnson a presidential ally like no

other (though LBJ continued the practice, begun by Kennedy, of wiretapping the phones of King and his associates).[6] The Johnson treatment, boxed in for years, reemerged in full force. Working through his old liberal collaborator and future vice president Hubert Humphrey, Johnson navigated the bill through the filibuster and signed it into law on July 2, 1964.

The Civil Rights Act was one of the landmark laws of the twentieth century, abolishing the segregation of public facilities that had been such a painfully obvious feature of American life. In effect, it restored and extended the Civil Rights Act of 1875, which had similar provisions, but which was struck down by the Supreme Court in 1882, precipitating the deep freeze in racial legislation that Johnson helped thaw in 1957. Now he had emerged as a pivotal figure for a truly meaningful change in American life. With dramatic speed, official segregation became a faint memory.

For Johnson, however, the Civil Rights Act was merely the opening salvo in what he planned as a brilliant display of legislative fireworks that have come to be known as "the Great Society." In January of 1964, he gave a famous State of the Union Address in which he declared "an unconditional war on poverty in America," a war that would lead to a blizzard of legislation beginning with the Economic Opportunity Act of 1964, which Johnson signed in August of 1964. He was positioning himself to win the presidency in his own right, and, given the Republicans' decision to nominate the seemingly Paleolithic conservative Barry Goldwater, Johnson's prospects were looking good.

There was, however, the irritant of the overseas situation in Vietnam, where Communist-backed forces in the North were trying to overrun a corrupt and wobbly government in the South. The situation had gnawed at Kennedy before he died, and it was not getting any better in the months since. Even as he was launching the War on Poverty, Johnson decided he needed to flank any moves Goldwater might make on his right. So when he sent naval patrols to probe the Gulf of Tonkin in the summer of 1964, and when Vietnamese Communists apparently attacked an American naval vessel—the key word, which haunts us to this day, is "apparently"—Johnson quickly went before Congress and jawboned his way to a resolution empowering him to respond as he saw fit. Having reinforced that conceivable chink in his armor, Johnson cruised to one of the great electoral victories of modern times—"Landslide Lyndon" was a term of irony no more—and prepared to embark on one of the most ambitious legislative programs in American history as he began his first term in his own right in January of 1965.

Johnson had apparently maneuvered the war in Vietnam out of the way for the time being, but the Civil Rights movement was not cooperating. Johnson felt, with some reason, that Civil Rights should go on the back burner in the aftermath of the 1964 law; politicians were loath to alienate a skittish white public by going too far too fast, and Johnson himself had a raft of other legislative priorities, many of which he rightly believed would help the poor and minorities. But if there was one lesson of the Civil Rights movement—a lesson King patiently explained to white ministers in his famous "Letter from Birmingham City Jail"—waiting for the right time would always be a losing proposition for those seeking racial equality. Having won the battle over segregation, activists prepared to move on to their next, perhaps decisive, objective: a stronger federal law protecting voting rights.

The right to vote may well be the most important of all in a democracy, the wellspring from which all else depends. Certainly, the white South could only cement its control over the region by disenfranchising African Americans, which it did with a plethora of grandfather clauses, poll taxes, literacy tests, and other impediments that prevented them from actually casting a ballot. When African Americans actually went to the polls, that is—there were other means, some involving white sheets, which made many black citizens disinclined to show up in the first place.

Voter registration drives had long been a fixture of the Civil Rights movement, notably in the work of leaders like Ella Baker and Bob Moses, who courageously led an often terrifying effort to register black voters in Mississippi in the early sixties. But in January of 1965, the principal battleground in this fight was Selma, Alabama, which activists had targeted as one of the most virulently racist cities in the South. A series of demonstrations and registration efforts were met with violent resistance by the notorious sheriff, Jim Clark, who used whips and cattle prods to beat back demonstrators, thousands of whom were jailed. To the disgust of many, particularly those in the rapidly radicalizing wing of the movement, Johnson held back from using federal force to protect them, fearing an even greater conflagration. But when one demonstrator was shot dead and a Unitarian minister was clubbed to death within days of each other, pressure to do something mounted.

And so it was that he swung into action. When Alabama governor George Wallace sought and was granted a meeting on March 13, Johnson went to work on him, poking and prodding a fellow Southerner in all the places he knew he'd be vulnerable. "Now listen, George," LBJ said to Wallace at the end of their meeting. "Don't think about 1968 [the next presidential election, in which Wallace himself would be a candidate]. Think about 1988. You and me we'll be dead and gone. . . . What do you want left after you when you die? Do you want a big marble monument that reads 'George Wallace—He Built?' Or do you want a little piece of pine board lying across that harsh caliche soil that reads, 'George Wallace—He Hated?'" Leaving the meeting, Wallace chuckled. "Hell, if I stayed there much longer he'd have me coming out for civil rights."[7]

The next day, Johnson asked permission from congressional leaders to address a joint session of Congress on the ensuing evening, the first such address of its kind in almost twenty years. He told presidential aide Richard Goodwin to write him a speech, and to be sure to mention Johnson's experiences working as a teacher of Mexican Americans as a young man. Johnson worked on the speech himself over the course of the following day, a day in which his wife noticed his spirits had lifted. He arrived at the Capitol the following evening greeting many old friends as a television audience of 70 million people listened to what he had to say.

"Many of the issues of civil rights are very complex and most difficult," Johnson conceded.

But about this there can and should be no argument: every American citizen must have an equal right to vote. There is no reason which can excuse the denial of that right. There is no duty which weighs more heavily on us than the duty we have to insure that right. Yet the harsh fact is that in many places in this country men and women are kept from voting simply because they are Negroes.

"Every device of which human ingenuity is capable, has been used to deny this right," the president asserted. But this has got to stop. That's why he demanded, after a century of such denials, that Congress pass a voting rights bill—immediately.

> But even if we pass this bill the battle will not be over. What happened in Selma is part of a far larger movement which reaches into every section and state of America. It is the effort of American Negroes to secure for themselves the full blessings of American life. Their cause must be our cause too. Because it's not just Negroes, but really it's all of us, who must over-come the crippling legacy of bigotry and injustice.
> And we shall overcome.[8]

Virtually every recollection and account of this speech em-phasizes the electrifying impact of these last four words. That the president of the United States would invoke the house hymn of the Civil Rights movement was a profound act of solidarity that was lost on no one (Johnson spoke the words slowly and for em-phasis). After a moment of eerie silence, the hall erupted in sus-tained applause. Martin Luther King, who had been invited to the speech but could not go—he had to deliver the eulogy for the fallen minister and could not get a flight in time—watched the speech on television. For the first time in the memory of his aides, they watched him cry.

As he stepped down from the platform and accepted congrat-ulations, Johnson made his way over to Emanuel Celler, the aged chairman of the House Judiciary Committee. "Manny, I want you to start hearings tonight," Johnson told him. When Cellar said he couldn't begin working on the bill until the following week, Johnson began jabbing at Cellar with his finger. "Start them *this* week, Manny. And hold night sessions, too."[9] And while the situation in Selma would remain tense for days to come, and there would be one more murder, federal marshals were on the scene to protect the marchers.

The Voting Rights bill would ultimately reach Johnson's desk on August 6, 1965. Its impact may well have been greater than that of the Civil Rights Act. By the end of 1967, every former Confederate state but Mississippi had more than half of its eligible black population registered to vote. By 1980, black and white registrations were nearly equal. In 1965, there had been a few hundred black officeholders in the United States; by 1989 the number had reached 6,000. Johnson had engineered an American Revolution.

Five days later, rioting broke out in what had been the relatively quiet black ghetto of Los Angeles. And even as he was ramming the Voting Rights bill through Congress, Johnson was secretly escalating the number of troops being sent to Vietnam. By 1968 this rising cataclysm would crush the man who had risen so high four years earlier. He threw in the towel, retired to his ranch, and grew his hair long just like the hippies he had placed under surveillance.

Lyndon Johnson had an extraordinary capacity for exploiting people. That never changed—even in the final years of his presidency, when his prestige went into a tailspin. The great drama of his career was to what ends he chose to exercise his tremendous capacity for manipulation. For much of his life the end was himself, and in moments like the 1948 Senate election, he behaved as an extraordinarily selfish man. But even when he was acting to enhance his own stature, Johnson could accomplish an extraordinary amount of good—amid the decidedly mixed record of the Great Society are a string of accomplishments in his presidency that, in large and small ways, remain fixtures of everyday life, among them Medicaid and Medicare, federal aid to education (from the preschool program Head Start to the gender-equity provisions of Title IX), the National Endowments of the Humanities and the Arts, the Corporation for Public Broadcasting, and much more. Certainly, each of these programs has its critics.

But they also have large and loyal constituencies and real track records of accomplishment—as Republicans would learn to their regret when they tried to take them down, largely without success, during the presidency of Bill Clinton.

Whatever his intentions and calculations, Johnson also made some huge mistakes. The biggest was the war in Vietnam, a war that destroyed countless lives and corroded the nation in ways that ranged from government deception to a polarizing public discourse that rent generations. In Johnson's own memorable words, "I left the woman I really loved—the Great Society—in order to get involved with that bitch of a war on the other side of the world." His decision to escalate the war in Vietnam is all the more awful for the fatalism with which he plunged deeper into a conflict he knew all along he could not win and yet could not afford to appear to lose. One might well have no choice but to regard this decision as unforgivable, though it should be said that Johnson's premises were by no means his alone—indeed, they were shared by a successor, Richard Nixon, who compounded LBJ's mistakes. To a great extent, Johnson's sins were American sins.

And yet Johnson was a notably, even uniquely, far-sighted politician. Perhaps the best illustration of this is his famous assertion, as he signed the Voting Rights Act, that "we are delivering the South to the Republicans for a generation."[10] That Johnson would do this cognizant of the consequences speaks to the intensity of his desire to distinguish himself (a kind of egotism, to be sure) as well as to what the great Johnson biographer Robert Caro has called his "savage determination" to champion civil rights (a kind of altruism, without a doubt). Johnson's prophecy came true. If the consequences have been painful, the fault is more ours than his.

*(previous page)* A FORD, NOT A LINCOLN: Gerald Ford, in an official White House photograph taken less than a month after taking office. The only chief executive never actually elected as part of a presidential ticket, Ford forfeited his popularity early in his brief term, but in so doing spared the nation further trauma in the aftermath of the Watergate scandal. (Presidential Portraits, Library of Congress)

## CHAPTER EIGHT

# VICE PRESIDENT FORD STUMBLES AT THE GATE

*In which we see a naïve man pardon a crook—and heal a nation*

On the morning of August 1, 1974, the relatively new White House chief of staff, Alexander Haig (he replaced H. R. Haldeman, who had resigned under the shadow of an indictment), came to see the even newer vice president, Gerald R. Ford (he replaced Spiro T. Agnew, who had also resigned under the shadow of an indictment) at the Executive Office Building adjacent to the White House. Haig had hoped for a private meeting, but Ford's chief of staff, Robert Hartmann—recognizing the tremendous political danger of having the chief aide for a man likely to be impeached or indicted in a private meeting with his potential successor—insisted on attending to make sure nothing untoward was said. An uneasy Haig explained that the scandal the country now knew as Watergate was growing. Recently discovered White House tapes documenting President Richard Nixon's involvement in the scandal would soon become public knowledge, contradicting what Nixon had been telling even his closest associates—among them Ford himself, who had genuinely believed

Nixon's denials of wrongdoing. With apparently little more to say, Haig left.

Shortly after noon, however, Haig called back, saying he wanted to see Ford again—alone. Haig returned to see the unsuspecting Ford and asked him if he was ready to become president "in a short period of time."[1] When Ford assured him he was, Haig went on to explain that Nixon and his lawyers were reviewing his options. Nixon could fight on, but if he was impeached and convicted, he would lose key perquisites like his pension. Another option was to resign.

Haig then came to the point: According to Article II, Section 2 of the U.S. Constitution, the President of the United States "shall have the power to grant Reprieves and Pardons for offenses against the United States, except in cases of Impeachment." Since no impeachment had yet taken place, Nixon, at least in theory, had the power to pardon himself and his Watergate conspirators and *then* resign. There was also the possibility, Haig suggested carefully and without attribution for the source of the idea, that Ford could pardon Nixon upon taking office. Was that Ford's reading of the situation? "Well Al," Ford replied, "I want some time to think," adding, as he always did when weighing important decisions, that he wanted to talk with his wife. The meeting ended.

When Ford revealed Haig's comments to Hartmann, his deputy was furious: There was no doubt in Hartmann's mind that Haig was acting at the direction of Nixon, who was sounding Ford out on a quid pro quo for the presidency. "I think you should have taken Haig by the scruff of the neck and the seat of the pants and thrown him the hell out of your office," he said. The irascible Hartmann was angry that Haig had lured Ford into such a meeting alone, without witnesses, so that no one could record or protect Ford from any future suggestion that he was in on a deal. Another close aide, Jack Marsh, agreed with Hartmann. Too trusting, even naïve, for his own good, Ford had been saddled with a time bomb that would virtually confirm any suspicions that the two men had cut a deal in the event Ford ever did issue a pardon.

Not that this seemed terribly likely. Ford himself had addressed the issue of a Nixon pardon the previous fall during his

confirmation hearings, responding to such a suggestion by saying, "I do not think the public would stand for it."[2] This was
sound judgment—judgment a good deal more sound than that
which led Ford to meet with Haig alone.

"I'm a Ford, not a Lincoln," he told his fellow countrymen
with characteristic modesty when he was in the process of being
selected vice president, the first step in an unexpected ascent to
the Oval Office.[3] It was a joke, but he was telling the truth, and
everyone knew it. Ford lacked the stature, the grace, and the talent of Lincoln, a man he admired greatly. But literally as well as
figuratively, he came from the same part of the world—or, to sustain the metaphor, he was simply a less sophisticated model assembled by the same manufacturer.

That part of the world was the Midwest. Ford actually was
born in Omaha, but his mother fled her abusive husband with her
infant son and ultimately settled down in Grand Rapids, Michigan, with a kindly paint salesman whose name the young child
adopted.[4] Despite these uncertain beginnings, Ford had in many
ways an archetypal childhood, graduating from high school as a
football star and attending the University of Michigan on an ath-
letic scholarship. After repeated rejection, he managed to get a
law degree from Yale before serving in the Navy during the Second World War. Upon returning home, he established a law
practice and then managed to defeat a corrupt isolationist Congressman in the Republican primary, assuring his election to the
seat. Not for the last time, Ford surprised skeptics.

This ability to exceed expectations was actually one of two
major themes in Ford's career. Whether as a student (at Michigan
he was considered a surprisingly good student—for a football
player), a congressman (Lyndon Johnson's cruel joke that Ford
"played too much football with his helmet off" echoed down
through the decades)[5] or even president (comedian Chevy Chase,
who rode to fame satirizing him, famously asserted that "President Ford kissed a snowball and threw a baby" in one of his *Saturday Night Live* "Weekend Update" newscasts),[6] Ford was
derided as a clumsy idiot. And yet his unassuming manner combined with a sense of implacable persistence and subtle insight to
impress anyone who took the time to observe him carefully.

Those who did knew there was no intellectual challenge he wasn't up to, and he moved up the congressional ladder with surprising speed, landing key committee appointments as well as other honors—Johnson himself, for example, appointed Ford as a member of the blue-ribbon Warren Commission that investigated the death of President Kennedy.

There was another factor, moreover, that operated in Ford's favor perhaps even more decisively, and that was his almost palpable sense of decency. He was not known as a particularly compelling speaker, or as a legislative innovator. But in terms of mastering the intricacies of a bill, counting votes among colleagues, staying in touch with the voters back home, or being a dependable repository of a compromise or confidence, Ford had no peer. "Oh, he was a likable fellow," remembered one Alabama Democrat. "And if he didn't know an issue, he would study it and ask questions until he did."[7] Known as a fiscal conservative strong on defense, Ford's positions were generally predictable, but disagreements with his colleagues were rarely personal.

Ford had one ambition that sustained him through thirteen consecutive terms in Congress: He wanted to become Speaker of the House. To that end, he declined a suggestion he move to the Senate in 1952, because he felt he was building enough seniority to reach his goal. In 1965, a group of friends in the House—among them Congressmen Donald Rumsfeld of Illinois and Richard Cheney of Wyoming—succeeded in electing Ford House Minority Leader. But all the goodwill and talent in the world would not make Ford Speaker of the House unless the Republicans were in the majority.

It was Ford's misfortune to be in Congress in an era—stretching from 1955 to 1995—of Democratic control of the lower chamber. There were times he had reason to be hopeful for a change, but those hopes were never realized. Ford was particularly optimistic in 1972, when the incumbent Republican—his old friend Dick Nixon, whom he had known since his arrival in Congress 24 years earlier—was cruising toward an easy reelection, raising hopes that his coattails would lead to GOP control of Congress. But the President lent little support to congressional races, and though he won by a gigantic majority, the Democrats retained control of both Houses. Chagrined, Ford decided he was tired of waiting. He told family and friends of his new plan: to run for reelection one more time in 1974, and then retire from public service in January of 1977. Then fate—or, more accurately, Nixon—intervened.

Strictly speaking, Ford's nomination for the vice presidency had nothing to do with Watergate. Spiro Agnew, who Nixon planned to dump anyway, had resigned in connection with bribery charges in October of 1973. Nixon had hoped to replace him with Texan John Connolly, a former Democrat, but widespread suspicions about Connolly, along with Nixon's weakened political position, forced him to accept the suggestion of congressional leaders, who considered Ford easy to confirm. As it turned out, however, the process turned out to be longer than anticipated. Some Democrats, seeing political blood in the water, wanted to defer Ford's confirmation hearings; if Nixon was forced from office, presidential succession would fall to House Speaker Carl Albert and thus control of the government would go to Democrats. Albert himself quashed such talk, however. Meanwhile, an exhaustive search into Ford's background showed him to be about as clean as any politician ever investigated (one major revelation: he had taken an improper tax deduction on a pair of suits he wore at the 1972 Republican National Convention). The Senate approved his confirmation 92–3 on November 27, and in the House the vote was 387–35 on December 6. An hour later Ford was sworn into office.

Over the course of the next eight months, Ford was on a tightrope. On the one hand, he was expected to be a loyal member of the Nixon administration. On the other, he was expected to distance himself from the Watergate scandal. One way he did this was by traveling widely—in fact, he covered 40 states and 100,000 miles giving talks at conventions, universities, and other public venues. Though he sometimes spoke in ambiguous, even contradictory ways when asked about Nixon, his popularity and profile grew. Before long even many Republicans believed the country would be better off with him, rather than Nixon, in charge. The question was whether, and how, Nixon would leave.

Nixon had hoped Ford would help clarify that. But whatever Haig or anyone else may have thought, Ford had gone into that August 1 meeting with an open mind, heard Haig out, and left to actively consider what he would do. Everyone—his wife Betty in particular—agreed that Ford should make no such deal. When Haig called that evening, Ford said, "I've talked it over with Betty, and we're prepared [for Ford to become President], but we can't get involved in the White House decision-making process." Haig said he understood: Nixon would have to make any decisions without the assurance that he would be protected from prosecution for his crimes. Just to be sure, Ford followed up with a phone call to Haig the next morning and asserted, "Nothing we talked about yesterday afternoon should be given any consideration in whatever decision the president may make."[8]

Nixon clung to power for another week. When Republican leaders from Congress went to him and told him he had to go, it was apparent, even to him, that he had little choice but to resign or be impeached. Finally, on August 8, he announced he would resign, effective the next day. After a maudlin farewell address to the White House staff, the Fords accompanied the Nixons to the plane that would take them home to San Clemente, California. Chief Justice of the Supreme Court Warren Burger, who had to be summoned from vacation in the Netherlands, then administered the oath of office to Ford. When it was over, Burger turned to Senate Minority Leader Hugh Scott and said, "Hugh, it [the Constitution] worked. Thank God, it worked." Ford, in a memorable line he insisted on using over the objections of aides, told his fellow Americans in a brief address that "our long national nightmare is over."[9]

In a sense, though, Ford's own nightmare was just beginning. It seemed that every time he turned around, it was Nixon, Nixon, Nixon. Reporters asking about him. Former Nixon aides (many of them, like Haig, still working in the White House with their primary loyalty to their former boss) trying to cart off sensitive documents to Nixon's home in San Clemente—a major headache for Ford, who was desperate to get rid of the evidence, but didn't want to do anything that would legally or politically implicate him. Even the White House staff seemed cowed in the shadow of

Nixon. Betty Ford was surprised when cooks and gardeners did not respond to her pleasantries, not realizing that the Nixons had issued strict orders during their tenure in the White House that such people were not to address the president or first lady.

Ford was particularly rattled by an August 28 press conference in which he was asked repeatedly if he was considering pardon and the broader implications of a trial of the former president. Thinking on his feet and trying to avoid committing himself, he said he "asked for prayers for guidance" on the matter. Yet he also said that he would not intervene in the legal process "until the matter reaches me."[10] This was at least partially a mixed message: Ford was saying he wanted a Nixon trial to go forward, but was also reserving the right to short-circuit it with a pardon. For Leon Jaworski, the special Watergate prosecutor, and John Sirica, the presiding judge in the Watergate trials, both mulling their options and hoping they wouldn't have to handle this hot potato, Ford's impromptu remarks were especially problematic. They were also instant front-page news.

"God dammit," Ford thought to himself after the session. "I am not going to put up with this. Every press conference from now on, regardless of the ground rules, will degenerate into a Q&A on 'Am I going to pardon Mr. Nixon.'" Buffeted by unanticipated pressures and his difficulty in sizing up appropriate questions and answers, Ford realized he really was clumsy. He now resolved to do something "to get that monkey off my back."[11]

It is a measure of Ford's integrity—and his poor political instincts—that he resolved to make the most important decision of his presidency alone. Two days after the August 28 press conference, he convened a meeting of his advisers. While he told them that that he still had not yet decided what he was going to do, he ordered them to investigate how—not whether—to execute a pardon for former President Nixon. Their reaction, which he did not silence, was cool. They questioned the timing, the public reaction, and they suggested that Ford should at least get an apology out of Nixon. "I can't argue with what you feel is right," one of his advisers told him. "But is this the right time?" Ford replied, "Will there *ever* be a right time?" (Actually, amid rumors of an ailing and severely depressed Nixon, Ford had some reason to think he had to act quickly lest it seem that the stress of his looming trial, and the failure to resolve it, would be perceived as hounding him to death.) Ford was mindful of his predecessors, particularly Lincoln, who issued the Emancipation Proclamation despite the resistance of his cabinet, and Harry Truman, who kept a sign on his desk, "The Buck Stops Here," that Ford had seen as a freshman in Congress.[12]

It's not clear when Ford resolved irrevocably to issue the pardon, but it took about a week to work out the plan, during which time the president made no overt moves to prepare the public. Nixon, correctly sensing a pardon was in the offing, refused to apologize for Watergate and the subsequent cover-up. But Ford took great solace in a 1915 Supreme Court ruling, in *United States v. Burdick*, that since a presidential pardon could be refused, acceptance was in itself a de facto admission of a crime. And so it was on Sunday, September 8, 1974, one month after Nixon had resigned, that Ford went before the American people and announced his decision. There were huge problems, he explained, on a simply procedural level in a trial of Richard Nixon, among them where to hold a trial and how to empanel an impartial jury. Assuming one could do this, it would take months if not years to get underway.

> During this long period of delay and potential litigation, ugly passions would again be aroused, our people would again be polarized in their opinions, and the credibility of our free institutions would again be challenged at home and abroad. In the end, the courts may well hold that Richard Nixon has been denied due process, and the verdict of history would be even more inconclusive.
>
> It is not the ultimate fate of Richard Nixon that most concerns me, though surely it deeply troubles every decent and compassionate person. My concern is the immediate future of this great country. . . .
>
> I do believe that the buck stops here, that I cannot rely on public opinion polls to tell me what is right. I do believe that

right makes might,[13] and that if I am wrong ten angels swearing I was right would not make any difference. I do believe
with all my heart and mind and spirit that I, not as President,
but as a humble servant of God, will receive justice without
mercy if I fail to show mercy.[14]

Public reaction was swift and decisive. Overnight, Ford's approval rating dropped from 71 percent to 49 percent—the greatest one-day drop ever recorded. His own press secretary, Jerry
terHorst, immediately resigned. "This blundering intervention is
a body blow to the President's own credibility and to the public's
reviving confidence in the integrity of its government," the *New
York Times* editorialized. The *Washington Post* called the act "nothing less than the continuation of a cover-up."[15] Republicans in the
House informed Ford that his decision would cost them seats in
the upcoming elections. Though this can't be proven as the reason for subsequent Democratic gains, it was probably true.

A few voices came forward in support. "The pardon is right,"
former vice president Hubert Humphrey, a liberal Democrat, asserted from China, where he was traveling. "It's the only decision
Ford could make." The following month, Watergate prosecutor
Jaworski gave an interview saying he agreed with the president's
decision. Ford himself decided to deal with the controversy
head-on, agreeing to something sitting presidents almost never
agree to do: testify before a congressional committee. When he
did so in October of 1974—again against the advice of some advisers—he candidly disclosed his meeting with Haig on August 1,
1974. Then and ever since, observers were absolutely certain that
Nixon and Ford had cut a deal.

Ford's lifelong reputation did gain him some credibility.
"Jerry was like a Boy Scout—the truth is the truth," Democrat
Peter Rodino of New Jersey, who chaired the House Judiciary
Committee, said at the time. "Any number of people felt there
had to be a deal, but they didn't know Jerry Ford."[16] And over
time, Ford's logic was vindicated: the extreme divisiveness over
Watergate (where, it should be said, a dismaying number of
Americans who heard Nixon assert "I am not a crook" were will-
ing to stand by him even after revelations of taped comments a

few days after the Watergate break-in proved that he was) began to abate.

Ford's pardon of Nixon permanently defined his presidency. A few other matters of importance happened on his watch, among them the 1975 collapse of South Vietnam's government in the aftermath of American withdrawal two years earlier. More hopeful was the furtherance of détente with the Soviet Union and the signing of the Helsinki Accords of 1975, in which the Soviets explicitly acknowledged human rights in their satellite nations. Ford engendered some sympathy by enduring two unsuccessful assassination attempts—a perhaps perverse affirmation of his legitimacy as a bona fide symbol of authority—but was increasingly at loggerheads with Congress, vetoing over 66 bills, largely in attempts to limit federal spending (54 of those vetoes were sustained). He held about twice as many press conferences as Nixon did in about half the time, but by January 1975, his approval rating had fallen to 37 percent. To a great degree, this was because Ford presided over a lagging economy. His attempts to deal with this largely took the form of exhortation; the WIN ("Whip Inflation Now") buttons his administration distributed became a source of widespread scorn.

And yet, for all of this, Ford decided he liked the job, could do it about as well as anyone else, and ran for reelection in 1976.[17] The odds were against him, not only because of lingering distaste over the pardon, but also because Watergate had discredited the Republican Party generally. Moreover, Ford faced a powerful challenge from within the GOP from Ronald Reagan, whose conservative backers were becoming more and more of a force to be reckoned with. The Democrats nominated an outsider, Georgia governor Jimmy Carter, who stressed his distance from establishment Washington. Despite all this, Ford came within a whisker of edging out victory in one of the closest elections in American history. Carter himself was widely reputed to be a man of uncommon decency and candor. And like Ford, he was pounded by congressional critics, the press, and restless voters who longed for larger-than-life leadership but railed at the excesses that invariably came with it. In the American presidency, it appears, nice guys finish last.

Other chapters in this book have paired the acts of men who served as president of the United States—acts of foolishness, pride, or short-sightedness juxtaposed with acts of wisdom, generosity, and vision. The actions in question were entirely separate, though they derived from the same source of character. So, for example, FDR's willfulness resulted in both the disastrous court-packing and a foresighted commitment to the Allies in a time of isolationism. The Johnson Treatment was the engine of the fraudulent 1948 Senate race as well as the redemptive Voting Rights Act. Even seemingly antithetical instincts, like Lincoln's oscillation between skepticism and faith, derived from the same lifelong inquiry about the source and legitimacy of moral authority in politics. But there's all the difference in the world between planting false accusations about a person and emancipating a race of people.

With Gerald Ford, the mistake and the achievement were the same act. Pardoning Richard Nixon was the right thing to do, even if he went about it the wrong way. Yet perhaps unique to all the people considered here, what was "wrong" with Ford's behavior was not the less attractive side of a multifaceted trait. His mistake was in thinking that other people were comparably as open as he was—and that people would understand his attempt to make a principled decision as just that. His errors were of tactics, not character.

His underlying judgment, however, was sound. Thoughtful people could and did disagree on the propriety of the Nixon pardon, and in fact there are aspects to the outcome that are undeniably unfair (all the president's accomplices went to jail, while Nixon wrote memoirs and rehabilitated his image to a remarkable degree that suggests something about the durable character of the unrepentant Nixon himself). But the judgment of history, insofar as it ever is, has been consistent on the value of Ford's decision. His paramount goal was to put the Watergate scandal not behind Nixon, not behind Gerald Ford, but behind the nation as a whole. And on that count he succeeded. In living out the precept of showing malice toward none, Ford truly was a Lincoln.

*(previous page)* STAR ATTRACTION: Ronald Reagan's official White House portrait, 1981. The former Hollywood actor and union organizer had a way of confusing reality with the movies, a tendency that pleased voters as well as resulted in felonies. But his faith in happy endings made a dream of ending the Cold War come true. (Presidential Portraits, Library of Congress)

## CHAPTER NINE

# "THE GIPPER" LOSES ONE

*In which we see a saber rattler break
some rules, get caught, and go on to win
an important contest—in good faith*

The story seemed too implausible to be true: An American agent named Robert McFarlane had secretly flown to Iran and negotiated a deal with officials from the regime of the Muslim fundamentalist Ayatollah Khomeini—the man responsible for the incarceration of 52 American hostages for 444 days between 1979 and 1981. Moreover, as part of that transaction, McFarlane authorized the shipment of sophisticated weapons to the regime on behalf of the President of the United States. Couldn't be. Not Ronald Reagan.

And yet the Lebanese journalist who heard the story knew that his sources were both reputable and well connected in Tehran. The story he wrote for his newspaper, *Al Shiraa*, focused primarily on factional infighting within the Khomeini regime. The bit about the American envoy, juicy as it was, was simply tacked on at the end.

Even as this story was being written in Beirut, two other American operatives, Marine Lt. Col. Oliver North and a former Air Force general turned arms merchant named Richard Secord, were briefly in the city. They were quietly negotiating the release of an American held hostage by an Islamic fundamentalist group. Their mission accomplished, McFarlane, Secord, and North boarded a helicopter bound for Cyprus as the first issues of *Al Shiraa* hit the city's newsstands.

It was Tuesday, November 4 in the United States—Election Day. President Ronald Reagan was on the stump, trying to convince the American people in this midterm election to keep his party in power in the U.S. Senate. (He failed.) Reporters following him on the campaign trail began asking: What's this we hear about a secret mission to Tehran? And this terror group Islamic Jihad: Is there any truth to the story that they released a hostage in response to "overtures" from the White House? Presidential spokesman Larry Speakes shrugged off such queries: He didn't know anything about it.

But more information kept leaking out. That very day, the Iranian speaker of the parliament, Ali Akbar Hashemi Rafsanjani, affirmed the *Al Shiraa* account, adding details that McFarlane had brought pistols, a Bible, and a cake decorated with a key. Two days later, the *Washington Post* and *Los Angeles Times* ran stories that there had been more than one such sale of weapons to Iran, that some of those sales had been conducted through Israeli intermediaries, and that Secretary of State George Shultz and Secretary of Defense Caspar Weinberger had expressed opposition to the policy but had been ignored ("this is almost too absurd to comment on," Weinberger had said to his aide, Colin Powell).[1] So the plans had proceeded without them.

One reason Weinberger regarded the scheme as absurd is that U.S.-Iranian relations were, officially at least, about as chilly as humanly possible. They had been so ever since Khomeini's fundamentalists had toppled the regime of the Shah of Iran, a staunch U.S. ally, and taken American hostages in 1978. Hostility between the two nations deepened in 1980 when Iran plunged into a bloody eight-year war with Iraq and the United States provided arms and other forms of support to Iraqi leader Saddam Hussein. That the United States government would even be communicating with Tehran, never mind selling arms, was a mind-boggling proposition for most Americans.

So was the notion that the Reagan administration—an administration with a well-established reputation for a hard line in international affairs—would be cutting deals with terrorist organizations. In fact, Reagan's very election was to a great extent the result of American impatience and frustration with the Carter administration's failure to secure the release of the 52 hostages seized in the aftermath of the Shah's entry into the United States for medical treatment in 1978. Reagan had called the situation "a humiliation and a disgrace." When finally forced to comment on the emerging reports, he asserted that his administration "did not, repeat, did *not* trade arms or anything else for hostages."[2]

The story got worse still. The arms sales to Iran, which began in 1985, had been conducted with a significant markup in price, creating profits from the transactions. These profits were funneled through a Swiss bank account to the anti-Communist guerrillas in Nicaragua known as the Contras, who were trying to overthrow the Communist government of the Sandinistas. Reagan had hailed the Contras as "freedom fighters" and "the moral equal of our founding fathers,"[3] but most observers saw them as typically brutal right-wing Latin American thugs of the kind the administration was also supporting in El Salvador, Guatemala, and Panama (where they happened to be in power rather than the rebels). Irritated by the administration's high handedness, Congress had passed a law in 1982, renewed two years later, specifically forbidding aid to the Contras. The operative overseeing the arms transfers, Col. North, had claimed that they were not illegal because they were not using congressionally appropriated funds. But selling government property and putting the profits anywhere but in the U.S. treasury was also illegal. Ironically, the administration had convinced Congress to overturn the law, and perfectly legal aid to the Contras was about to resume. It was only in the closing weeks of the so-called Democracy Project that its cover had been blown, first when the Sandinistas shot down an American plane carrying weapons to the Contras (the one survivor, an American operative named Eugene Hasenfus, was captured and confessed to his captors), and then with the more damaging publication of the *Al Shiraa* story.

And to top it all off, there was a cover-up. As the story began to get out and Reagan's attorney general, Edwin Meese, began reluctantly to investigate—it was Meese who disclosed the Contra side of what came to be known as the Iran-Contra affair—Oliver North and his secretary, Fawn Hall, conducted a "shredding party" to destroy relevant documents. When the shredder got jammed, Hall stuffed documents into her clothes and boots and secreted them away to another machine. What neither they nor the other major player in the operation, National Security Adviser Admiral John Poindexter, failed to realize, however, is that White House computers had back-up files for all those being tossed or erased. In the days to come much of the whole sordid affair would come to light.

The question everyone wanted answered, of course, was the same one people asked during Watergate: What did the president know and when did he know it? In the case of Richard Nixon, the answers were "everything" and "almost immediately," and with just about any other president the answers would presumably be the same in the case of the Iran-Contra Affair. But the very things President Reagan's critics complained most insistently about—his detached, even disconnected, management style—actually worked in his favor here: It was not hard to believe he was clueless. Reagan himself cheerfully contributed to this impression. "It's true hard work never killed anybody, but I figure, why take the chance?" he once joked.[4]

In the winter of 1986–87, however, no one at the White House was laughing. Reagan reputedly turned white when told about the Contra side of the affair, though it was unclear whether this was a matter of shock or guilt. The president named a special review panel to investigate the affair under the leadership of former Texas Senator John Tower, but when Reagan himself testified in January of 1987, his answers were embarrassing recitations of irrelevant anecdotes coupled with a professed inability to remember the most relevant details. The Tower Commission exonerated Reagan of committing a crime, but described the president as remote, uninformed, and easily manipulated. After the report was released, Reagan went on television to render something resembling an apology. "I told the American people I did not trade arms for hostages. My heart and best intentions still tell me this is true, but the facts and the evidence tell me it is not."[5]

This wasn't quite the end of it. Congress held hearings in the summer of 1987, and a special prosecutor investigating the affair ultimately brought fourteen indictments, gaining eleven convictions, including McFarlane (who unsuccessfully attempted to commit suicide), Poindexter and North (whose convictions were overturned because they were based on testimony for which they had received immunity for the congressional hearings), and Secord (who pleaded guilty and was sentenced to two years' probation). Reagan's successor, George H. W. Bush, pardoned six other defendants, among them McFarlane, at the end of his own presidency. Bush's own knowledge, or lack thereof, as vice president had been a campaign issue, but not one that prevented him from getting elected president in 1988.

Unlike Richard Nixon, Reagan proved too personally popular with the American people to face impeachment. Democratic congresswoman Patricia Schroeder of Colorado, bemused by Reagan's ability to simply ignore the considerable criticism he received, had dubbed him "the Teflon President."[6] But the Iran-Contra Affair damaged the standing of an administration that for six years had seemed unstoppable. Perhaps more important, it seemed like a jarring interruption of a powerful personal storyline which, if never entirely accepted by all of the American people, nevertheless was part of a Reagan myth embraced by the people around him as well as the people at large. Now, suddenly, the resolution of that storyline was in question.

In his now-classic 1987 study *Reagan's America*, Garry Wills notes that Ronald Reagan once described his childhood as "one of those Huck Finn–Tom Sawyer idylls" without acknowledging the dark subtext of racism, superstition, and crime that lace through those books and Twain's fiction generally.[7] In this regard, Wills notes, Reagan was typical of many of his contemporaries who thought of *Huckleberry Finn* as children's literature. He was also typifying a pattern of prettifying unpleasant realities that would characterize Reagan's own life. Reagan's father, Jack, was an Irish Catholic alcoholic shoe salesman; his mother, Nelle, was a pious Disciple of Christ evangelical Protestant (his older brother Neil became a Catholic, while Reagan himself was baptized in his mother's faith). This cultural and psychological fault line in what was nevertheless a loving family appears to have resulted in a distinctive Anglo-Celtic blend in Reagan's character—a combination of dignity and charm. His childhood under the shadow of an alcoholic may also explain, as some have speculated, an eager, even compensatory, cheerfulness.

Despite these early challenges, and despite coming of age in the depths of the Great Depression—Reagan was a passionate FDR devotee—much of his early life seemed to unfold like an effortless American Dream: Midwestern summers as a lifeguard who saved the lives of dozens of people; social success as an undergrad at Eureka College in Illinois; a burgeoning career as a sportscaster in Iowa; and an impulsive screen test that landed him a contract as a B-list movie star (his best-known role was as Notre Dame football star George Gipp; hence his nickname "The Gipper"). His first marriage to actress Jane Wyman didn't work out; but his subsequent bond with another, Nancy Davis, proved durable (he had children from both marriages).[8] In 1947 Reagan was elected president of the Screen Actor's Guild, but his growing suspicion of the Soviet Union at the dawn of the Cold War trumped his commitment to labor politics, and he served as an informer for the House Un-American Activities Committee investigating Communist influences in Hollywood. By the mid-fifties he had largely completed his transformation from a New Deal Democrat to a country-club Republican.

After giving a legendary speech for Republican presidential candidate Barry Goldwater in 1964, Reagan decided to run for governor of California in 1966. The popular Democratic incumbent, Edmund "Pat" Brown, was running for his third term, the first of a series of opponents who could not bring himself to take Reagan seriously. Reagan, for his part, cheerfully admitted his inexperience, which he viewed as an asset. Ultimately, he was correct, winning the race by a decisive margin. As such, he was viewed as a national symbol of the rising unrest with Lyndon Johnson's Great Society. By 1968 Reagan was being discussed as presidential timber, albeit as a long-shot. Nixon was the presumed nominee in 1972, but by 1976 Reagan had developed sufficient strength to mount a powerful challenge to President Ford, who barely got the nomination. In 1980, Reagan dispatched his only serious contender, George Bush (who dubbed Reagan's plan to cut taxes and raise defense spending "voodoo economics"),[9] and then cemented his control of the Republican Party by making Bush his running mate.

Nevertheless, there remained serious questions about whether Reagan could really be elected President of the United States in 1980. Even some of the people who liked him had a hard time shaking the notion that he was an amiable dunce, and those who disliked him feared he would blunder into nuclear war. Reagan also sent a truly awful message in choosing to kick off his presidential campaign in Philadelphia, Mississippi, the place where three Civil Rights workers had been murdered in 1964, as part of an effort to appeal to white racists who had historically clung to the Democrats but were now leaving them in droves. Politics aside, there were concerns that Reagan, who at 69 was the oldest candidate in American history, was simply not up to the job.

Yet in one of those great paradoxes of American history, Reagan projected a greater sense of vigor than the younger Carter. In the end, a desire to change a society marked by pervasive economic, social, and political malaise prevailed, and the margin of Reagan's victory—51 percent to 41 percent, with 6 percent for the former liberal Republican John Anderson—surprised many (Reagan took a commanding 489 electoral votes to Carter's 49). The improbable had become inevitable.

Perhaps ironically, the catalyst for Reagan's success was a terrifying setback: the assassination attempt of March 1981 that left him and a number of aides critically injured (far more injured, in fact, than the public was allowed to realize at the time). In this crucial hour of crisis, with a bullet an inch from his heart, Reagan's essential character shone through. Anxious for his wife as he headed to the hospital, he greeted her upon arrival by saying,

"Honey, I forgot to duck." In the operating room, he responded to a surgeon who explained he was about to operate by saying, "I hope you're all Republicans." The surgeon responded by saying "Today, Mr. President, we are all Republicans."[10]

And long after, too: The outpouring of support Reagan received during his convalescence provided a crucial measure of political support as his political program passed into law. Well, sort of: Reagan got his tax cuts, but Democrats fended off many of the spending cuts, with the result that the U.S. government began running the huge budget deficits that have bedeviled it ever since. Yet the dominant impression was one of Reagan's political strength, an impression that was reinforced in the summer of 1981 when he broke a strike of air traffic controllers by firing them all—an important turning point in the history of labor in the United States. By 1983, the economy was beginning to improve, in large measure because the draconian interest rate hikes imposed by Federal Reserve Chairman Paul Volker in 1979–81 brought rampant inflation under control. Reagan ran for reelection in 1984 amid a surge in optimism through much of American society that seemingly erased the dark mood of the early eighties, and one that was expertly stage-managed by handlers who used slogans like "Morning in America" and sun-drenched images of Reagan on horseback to package their candidate. Reagan's opponent, Walter Mondale, a Hubert Humphrey protégé who flatly admitted he planned to raise taxes, never had a chance—except during their first debate, when Reagan seemed dangerously disconnected. The 72-year-old Reagan bounced back in their next encounter by joking that he was not going to allow Mondale's youth to be used against him, and never looked back, winning 49 states in the worst electoral drubbing the Democrats ever received.

In the famous formulation of philosopher Isaiah Berlin, who distinguished between the fox who knows many things but the hedgehog who knows one big thing, Reagan was the quintessential hedgehog, albeit one who knew two things. One was that Big Government was bad, and Reagan focused on this truth—as he understood it—to the exclusion of just about everything else in domestic policy. The other thing he knew was that the United

States had to reassert its place in the world, to recover the sense of authority it had lost in the wake of defeat in Vietnam, humiliation in the Middle East, and even challenges in its own Latin American backyard.

Reagan demonstrated his willingness to do this in a number of ways. One obvious manifestation was in his strong desire to overthrow the Sandinista regime Carter had tolerated, and his invasion of the tiny Caribbean island of Grenada, which he justified with questionable claims of rescuing American medical students from a Marxist regime. Another clear signal was massive military buildup, typified by the replacement of older nuclear weapons with new Pershing II and MX missiles, the latter nicknamed (in what some would call an Orwellian touch) "peacekeepers." These moves sparked a new antinuclear movement in Europe and the United States. At the same time, however, the downing of a Korean civilian aircraft that had wandered into Soviet airspace by a Soviet fighter plane in 1983 demonstrated that the Kremlin would brook no challenges to its territorial prerogatives.

Reagan, for his part, intensified his rhetoric to match his actions. He appalled liberals and even many diplomats in a notorious speech he gave to the National Association of Evangelicals in 1983. "In your discussions of the nuclear freeze proposals, I urge you to beware the temptation of pride—the temptation of blithely declaring yourselves above it all and label both sides equally at fault, to ignore the facts of history and the aggressive impulses of an evil empire,"[11] he said. For years to come, Reagan's opponents would invoke the phrase "evil empire" to mock his crudity and ignorance. This perception of crudity and ignorance was intensified the following year when, while preparing for a radio address with what he thought was a dead microphone, he joked, "My fellow Americans, I am pleased to tell you I just signed legislation which outlaws Russia forever. The bombing will begin in five minutes."[12]

As far as his opponents were concerned, the ultimate expression of Reagan's descent into unreality, however, came in 1983, when he announced, with great fanfare, his plans to develop a Strategic Defense Initiative (SDI), popularly dubbed "Star

Wars." If implemented, this would represent a revolutionary—
and highly destabilizing—development in the dynamics of the
Cold War, not only because it would represent an abrogation of
the Strategic Arms Limitation Treaty the Nixon administration
had signed in 1972, but even more so because it would mean the
United States had the ability to destroy incoming nuclear missiles, thus upending the doctrine of Mutually Assured Destruction (MAD) that had governed Cold War thinking for decades.
Other critics considered SDI highly unrealistic, because it if was
less than 100 percent effective MAD in fact would remain in
place despite the appalling costs of SDI implementation. In fact,
of course, relatively little was accomplished on SDI during Reagan's presidency (the program is still under development in test-
ing stations in Alaska and the Pacific). But its mere potential
upended many basic assumptions people around the world had
been living with for many years.

   In a sense, of course, the most important reaction was not
that of Reagan's supporters or critics at home, or third parties
abroad, but the leaders of the Soviet Union. We now know they
were very worried indeed. Even without SDI, the atrophying
regime was acutely aware of its growing inability to match the
U.S. military buildup launched by Reagan. Even increasingly
commonplace technology in the United States like personal
computers and photocopiers heightened its insecurities about
falling behind on the one hand and the political dangers involved
in allowing their citizens access to such resources on the other.
The government was reputedly in panic in 1983 when a NATO
exercise code-named ABLE ARCHER was almost viewed as a
genuine nuclear attack. These problems were exacerbated by its
painfully sclerotic leadership for much of the 1980s. Leonid
Brezhnev's death in 1982 led to his replacement by former KGB
chief Yuri Andropov and upon his death two years later by
Kostantin Chernenko—three men who made the equestrian
Reagan seem positively boyish by comparison.

   And then came Mikhail Gorbachev. Fifty-four years old when
he became general secretary of the Communist Party in 1985,
Gorbachev was determined to revitalize the USSR. The steps he
took toward this end included "perestroika" (restructuring), es-

sentially a decentralization and promotion of private enterprise; "glastnost" (openness), a new emphasis on free speech and openness; a crackdown on the alcoholism that ran rampant through much of Russia and its satellite republics; and a managed withdrawal from its Vietnam-like war in Afghanistan, which had been severely sapping the government's resources and legitimacy. Gorbachev, who had traveled widely and impressed leaders like Britain's Margaret Thatcher before becoming the leader of the USSR, also sought better relations with the West and was particularly interested in cutting military expenditures by fostering a better relationship with the United States.

While Gorbachev represented a new kind of leader for the Soviet Union, the possibilities his leadership portended would ultimately depend a great deal on Reagan's reaction to him. The initial indications were not especially promising. The two leaders met for the first time in Geneva in November of 1985, a meeting that the sometimes inattentive Reagan prepared for meticulously. Though there were moments in which the two seemed to connect on a personal level—"I at once felt him to be a very authentic human being," Gorbachev said years later[13]—their talks were inconclusive (most of the media attention seemed to focus on the notably less cordial relationship between the two mens' wives). Gorbachev insisted on Reagan modifying his commitment to SDI, while Reagan, offering to share the technology, would not be disenthralled from his attachment to it. The two did, however, agree to meet again in each other's countries.

Their next meeting, in Reykjavik, Iceland, in October of 1986 had a slapdash quality: the plans did not come together until relatively late, and was meant as a planning session for a more substantial summit to be held in the United States. With some excitement, the two leaders grappled with a package of proposals with the promise of reducing a variety of classes of nuclear weapons by 50 percent. Once again, however, their conversation foundered on SDI—Reagan wouldn't budge, and Gorbachev didn't believe his promise to share it. Yet the very candor and irritation of their conversations suggested a productive sense of engagement. Gorbachev made clear he wasn't even going to pretend that the Soviets would try to keep up with SDI, and indicated

some willingness to allow laboratory work on it. Late in the negotiations, with their respective planes on the runways, Reagan suddenly made a dramatic proposal: Let's move beyond limiting
nuclear weapons, or even reducing them. How about agreeing,
right here, right now, to eliminating them entirely from Europe as
the first step toward complete disarmament?

This was a proposal of breathtaking audaciousness. Over the
years, the Soviets had made similar proposals, but they had
never been taken especially seriously, since Russian troops were
poised to overrun the continent and nuclear weapons were the
principal deterrent the United States had at its disposal. Now
Reagan was offering to toss this advantage away. The tension
was tremendous, as the cautious Soviet leader agreed—but, he
added, "This all depends, of course, on you giving up SDI."
Reagan, angered by a stipulation he regarded as non-negotiable,
got up and left. "Goddammit," he told his chief of staff, Don
Regan, as the motorcade began to move, "we were *that* close to
an agreement."

This was precisely what some of Reagan's closest advisers had
feared—indeed, he gave some of them the scare of their lives. To
some degree, this anxiety was the result of some ambiguity about
just what the Reagan had proposed. "Mr. President, we've got to
clear up this business of you agreeing to get rid of nuclear
weapons," John Poindexter, who accompanied Reagan to the
summit, said to him in trying to sort out what had happened.
"But John," Reagan replied, "I did agree to that." Poindexter,
persisting, said, "No, you couldn't have." Answered Reagan:
"John, I was there and I did." (Contrary to the image of Reagan
as a wooden marionette, accounts of the summit suggest he was
very much in charge.)[14]

As details of the summit came out, some conservatives expressed disgust. One conservative columnist, George Will,
charged that Reagan was accelerating the "moral disarmament of
the west by elevating wishful thinking to the status of a political
philosophy." Howard Philips, head of the Conservative Caucus,
called Reagan "a useful idiot" for the Soviets.[15]

By any conventional reckoning, the Rekjavik summit was a
failure. In an important sense, however, it revealed a dramatic

evolution in Reagan's vision: a willingness to act on his perceived sense of leverage and actually pursue peace with his opponent. There was genuine courage in that stand: So many Cold Warriors had been so hostile for so long that many regarded any de-escalation as naïve folly. Hostility could be accepted, even normalized. But actually paring back the destructive power of nuclear weapons seemed difficult for even many liberals to credibly imagine.

Where did this willingness come from? Here we come to a crucial point in the story, where the Reagan-Gorbachev relationship intersects with the Iran-Contra Affair. Some observers have speculated that Nancy Reagan had been pushing her husband to work toward a substantial legacy in superpower relations once he won a second term in 1984. It was also believed at the time that Reagan's behavior at Rejkjavik was rooted in hopes for a diplomatic breakthrough as a bauble for the voters in the upcoming midterm elections in 1986. These two imperatives both took root earlier than, and were separate from, the Iran-Contra Affair. But the key fact here is that the Rejkjavik summit occurred just as Iran-Contra was bubbling up in national consciousness—Eugene Hasenfus, the pilot captured by the Sandinistas, was making headlines just before Rejkjavik, while the *Al Shiraa* story broke in November, just after Rejkjavik. Reagan's intensifying engagement with Gorbachev once Iran-Contra became a gigantic media event was widely understood as central to—even inextricable from—the effort to repair the damage the scandal had done to his reputation.

Repairing that damage was a matter of public relations, but it had important policy ramifications as well. A good example was the replacement of some of Reagan's advisers late in his second term, in large part to demonstrate that the president was turning over a new leaf in the wake of Iran-Contra. (Also, one major figure in hatching the scheme, CIA Director William Casey, had died.) A number of the new appointees, among them Colin Powell as National Security Adviser, counseled a more engaged approach to the Soviets than his suspicious mentor, Caspar Weinberger. A recognition of failure in one policy sowed the seeds of success in another.

The Reagan-Gorbachev effort to accomplish something substantive finally bore fruit in 1987, when the two leaders agreed to abolish intermediate range nuclear missiles from Europe. Though this was far more modest than Reagan's impulsive proposal at Rekjavik, and represented only a small part of their arsenals, it was the first time the United States and the Soviet Union had agreed to actually reduce the number of nuclear warheads. The agreement was particularly notable because the Soviets had dropped their insistence that the United States abandon SDI. Gorbachev came to the United States to sign the treaty, and charmed American citizens with impulsive acts like stopping his limousine in downtown Washington, D.C., to shake hands with them. Reagan was not intimidated by Gorbachev's appeal. "I don't resent his popularity," he explained. "Good Lord, I co-starred with Errol Flynn once."[16] The love fest continued in 1988 when Reagan made a trip to Moscow as he finished up his presidency. When asked if he still regarded the Soviets as "the focus of evil in the modern world," he replied, "They've changed." So had he.

Gorbachev, for his part, continued ruling the Soviet empire. One of his most important objectives was to liberate Russia from the impossibly onerous task of supporting its satellite states, which were now encouraged to manage their own affairs. Yet this proved to be the tipping point in the Soviet Union's ability to survive its own internal contradictions. Within a year of Reagan's departure from office, the Berlin Wall he had once demanded Gorbachev tear down was in tatters, not because of anything Gorbachev had done directly, but because the people of East Germany—and Poland, and Hungary, and a number of other places—insisted on their freedom. In 1991 Gorbachev himself would soon be consigned to political oblivion, first by being put under house arrest as part of a reactionary coup, and then being supplanted by the man who faced down that coup, Boris Yeltsin.

By that point, Reagan had begun a lonely journey into Alzheimer's disease. It requires no great speculation to imagine that this malady had begun stealing into his consciousness even during his presidency. Long before he died in 2004, he had already disappeared. But, of course, he had always been a notably elusive figure.

In retrospect, we can now see that the Iran-Contra Affair was a true turning point in U.S. foreign policy, the nexus of the two great international challenges the nation has faced since the end of the Second World War: the Cold War and the struggle we have come to know as the War on Terror. Illegality aside, Iran-Contra was a failure on both fronts: It neither achieved the immediate goal of dislodging the Sandinistas from power (they were eventually voted out of office, itself a measure of their relative legitimacy, particularly compared to the right-wing alternatives), nor did it address the longer-term problem of Middle Eastern enemies from taking hostages and other forms of what military strategists call "asymmetrical warfare." Of course, no president since Reagan has had much luck on this front, either.

The real surprise is that Reagan was able to salvage the re-maining fragment of his presidency by making bona fide head-way with a Cold War he had waged without regard to borders, legal or geographic. Even more surprising was the way he achieved something: by reaching out as a man of peace. The con-ventional political wisdom of the 1970s held that only Nixon could go to China. But perhaps only Reagan could go to the So-viet Union the way he did in the late 1980s. Reagan did not, sin-gle-handedly, end the Cold War: There are too many people on either side of the Iron Curtain who deserve credit for that, among them Pope John Paul I, the Solidarity movement in Poland, and the thousands of Eastern Europeans at the Berlin Wall who voted with their feet in rejecting Soviet tyranny. But it is only fair that those who were among his greatest skeptics ac-knowledge his pivotal role. Reagan did not pay attention to a lot of things, to the detriment of many people. But this was one thing he did. And whether we want to admit it or not, the man who terrified skeptics around the world with his perceived rigid-ity and recklessness ended his career by making the world a safer place. The goal never changed. But the means did, and that made all the difference.

In an important sense, we continue to live, for better and worse, in the Age of Reagan. The skepticism about big government that he expressed continues to be, in effect, the default setting of American politics. And while the events of September 11, 2001, mark a historical watershed, the fact remains that the formidable challenges the War on Terror pose are simply less awful in scale than the murderous proxy wars and the specter of mutually assured destruction the Cold War once posed. Moreover, the response to the War on Terror is framed in Cold War terms, sometimes in ways that were as dubious then as they are now (such as President Bush's 2001 assertion, "You're either with us or against us in the fight against terror").[17] No politician since Reagan has successfully changed the basic equations as he formulated them.

Sooner or later, one will. It also seems likely that sooner or later we will once again be faced with threats truly on the scale of the kind Reagan and his generation was forced to grapple with. In that case, Reagan's legacy may best be understood not in terms of his considerable achievements and mistakes, but from the exceptionally powerful and bright spirit he brought to American life. At its best, this spirit was not one of denial, but rather an avowed embrace of hope. In his eulogy for his father, Reagan's son Ron—a man of a decidedly different political temperament—captured this hope:

He was, as you know, a famously optimistic man. Sometimes such optimism leads you to see the world as you wish it were as opposed to how it really is. At a certain point in his presidency, Dad decided he was going to revive the thumbs-up gesture. So he went all over the country, of course, giving everybody the thumbs up. Dory [Ron Reagan's wife, Doria] and I found ourselves in the presidential limousine one day returning from some big event. My mother was there and Dad was, of course, thumbs-upping the crowd along the way. And suddenly, looming in the window on his side of the car, was this snarling face. This fellow was reviving an entirely different hand gesture and hoisted an entirely different digit in our direction. Dad saw this and without missing a beat turned to us and said, "You see? I think it's catching on."[18]

That was the thing about Reagan: Even when you disagreed with him—even when you knew in your heart he was wrong—the man was irresistible.

*(previous page)* BILL OF HEALTH: William Jefferson Clinton, official White House photo, 1992. The major legislative initiative of his presidency, health care reform, failed, but Clinton found a new lease on life in checking the excesses of a conservative movement that failed to perceive the limits of Americans' desire for limited government. (Presidential Portraits, Library of Congress)

## CHAPTER TEN

# "SLICK WILLIE" SLIPS AND FALLS

*In which we see an offensive player master a defensive strategy*

The conventional wisdom—a view held from the day he declared he was running for president in 1991 to the day he left office a decade later—was that Bill Clinton's sex life was not especially relevant to how he did his job. This was the view of primary voters, the majority that elected him twice, public opinion survey respondents, and the United States Senate, which declined to convict him in his 1999 impeachment. Actually, even many of Clinton's most severe critics did not argue with his sexual escapades in themselves—of which, it needs to be clear at the outset, there were many more than the explosive Monica Lewinsky scandal. (As with the much more grave crisis of Watergate, that liaison was only the tip of an ethical iceberg.) It was lying about his actions under oath, not the actions themselves, that most of his critics considered the legally punishable offense, though it should be said that there were people across the political spectrum that believed that he was criminally guilty of sexual harassment. Yet few of these people argued that Clinton's behavior, however abhorrent, had much bearing on how he handled, say, Arab-Israeli relations.

In fact, Clinton's private behavior was deeply, if silently, en-twined with many aspects of his presidency. Even if one assumes that he could perfectly manage telephone conversations with congressmen while engaged in sexual acts (as alleged in the re-port of Independent Prosecutor Kenneth Starr),[1] it is clear that Clinton's private life did indeed affect his job—or, at least per-ceptions of his job. Perhaps the best example is the mood of sus-picion that surrounded Clinton's limited and unsuccessful attempts to strike at the terrorist camps of Osama bin Laden in 1998, a move widely dismissed as a wag-the-dog subterfuge de-signed to distract the public from his political problems at home. Clinton's private behavior raised questions about his credibility that in turn affected perceptions of his public motives, and while it may be incorrect, even unfair, to blame him for suspicions that may well have been unfounded, everyone understands that effec-tiveness—broadly and vaguely defined, to be sure—is one of the indispensable prerequisites of success in politics.

But the insidious influence of Clinton's sexuality was not solely a passive force. It also shaped the most important, con-sidered, and even cherished decisions Clinton made in office. The best example of this may be his failed health care initiative, whose questionable timing, and delegation to his wife, appears to have been in part an act of personal atonement for marital infidelity.

In some ways, health care—or, more specifically, govern-ment-provided medical services through an insurance program— had become the Holy Grail of Democratic politics. President Roosevelt had originally envisioned it as a component of the So-cial Security Act, but it was jettisoned amid a welter of competing political pressures. His successor, Harry Truman, actually intro-duced legislation to create a national, single-payer health care system, but the proposal, attacked by the American Medical As-sociation as virtually communistic, never gained traction. Lyn-don Johnson did succeed in getting coverage for the elderly (through Medicare) and the poor (through Medicaid, an after-thought that has become a huge item in the federal budget), but that's because he was helping people the private sector wasn't much interested in as a source of profit.

By the 1990s, that private sector in health care—particularly health insurance companies that moved away from traditional fee-for-service models toward a newer one of "managed care" through "health maintenance organizations" (HMOs)—had grown dramatically in its scope and power to shape the welfare and choices of individual Americans. The U.S. health care system was widely viewed as the best in the world in terms of state-of-the-art care, but the very capitalistic motives that spurred innovation also imposed costs that increasingly priced the poor and even the middle class from access to the system. In fact, by the time Clinton became president, some 37 million people, 20 percent of the U.S. population, lacked insurance, and many of those who had it lived in fear that their coverage was inadequate or could be denied.

Although he was vague on the details, Clinton had run for president promising to "take on the health care profiteers and make health care affordable for every family."[2] His campaign advisers described an approach of "managed competition," which would preserve the private sector as the primary source of most health insurance, with universal coverage of the entire U.S. population attained through a more assertive supplemental and regulatory role on the part of the federal government. By the time he took office in 1993, this initiative was near the top of his priorities.

As is true of every president, however, priorities, and strategies for realizing them, often conflict. Clinton dearly wanted to launch new initiatives, particularly in health care, but he also wanted—needed—to show he was a sober steward for the nation's financial resources, particularly since the ballooning federal deficit had been such a large issue in the presidential campaign (it had been the foundation of insurgent Ross Perot's hugely successful third-party candidacy). Many voters seemed receptive to health care reform, but had identified it as the third most important issue after the state of the economy and the budget deficit. Clinton came into office knowing that the national debt would constrain him in a way it did not, say, Lyndon Johnson, but was dismayed to be told by some of his economic advisers that the deficit situation was far more dire than he realized. Reluctantly accepting their advice, he trimmed his sails on a proposed spending package to stimulate the economy ("You mean to tell me that the success of the program and my re-election hinges on the federal reserve and a bunch of fucking bond traders?" he famously asked at one point)[3] and raised taxes with a 1993 budget that narrowly passed amid Republican accusations that it would damage the economy.

From the start, it was clear that Clinton's wife, Hillary, an accomplished policy analyst who had reformed the Arkansas educational system while Clinton was governor, would lead the health care initiative. And she was chomping at the bit to get started. But amid the array of competing priorities—Vice President Gore in particular emerged as a competitor for the president's ear—Clinton scuttled the plan, much desired by Hillary, to introduce the health care plan immediately. In the aftermath of a bruising campaign that included revelations of his waywardness, she had reason to smolder.

Trimming his economic aspirations was an act of political retrenchment, but Clinton was eager to go on offense against the conservative Republicans who stood in his way. The question, again, was how. Some of his advisers urged him to act on a campaign promise to reform the welfare system, which was widely criticized by conservatives and even many liberals as inefficient and misplaced in terms of priorities and incentives. These advisers noted that the bipartisan support for such a move made it more likely to be successful and thus build up a store of political capital that Clinton could then spend on the health care initiative. Others, however, noted that presidential mandates are strongest at the start of a new term, and these are the times to make the biggest push. Such a view had legitimacy; it was also true, however, that Clinton came into office by winning a three-way race with only 43 percent of the popular vote. It is probably impossible to calculate just how important Hillary—and the desire to please her for reasons that may not have wholly been pure—was in Clinton's decision to attack health care first. But it strains credulity to think payback was not part of his calculus.

From the start, however, Clinton's plan was beset with obstacles. Notoriously undisciplined, the administration failed to impose order on the internal bickering and irresolution that delayed the plan far beyond the promised 100 days. The man who handled many of the details of the plan, the Clintons' old friend Ira Magaziner, proved to be an irascible and divisive figure. The whole project was cloaked in secrecy, with many key constituencies (particularly health insurance companies) frozen out, raising suspicions and hostility.

The plan itself was also problematic. Highly complex, it relied on managed competition in the form of large regional alliances that would be able to bargain with health care providers to keep prices down and a system of "community rating" that would achieve universal coverage in part by barring insurers from penalizing people with risk factors like age or preexisting conditions. The bill itself ran to over 1,300 pages, a fact that critics seized upon as evidence of its Byzantine quality (though Clinton noted in his memoirs that Congress routinely passes bills of such length). It also faced competition from alternative proposals that ran the gamut from tax breaks for individuals who were willing to insure themselves to a Canadian-style single-payer system that eliminated the private sector entirely.

Clinton forged ahead, urged on by Hillary, who pushed for an aggressive stance against skeptics and avowed opponents of the plan. Clinton unveiled the plan in his State of the Union Address in January of 1994, defiantly brandishing a pen and telling Congress that "if you send me legislation that does not guarantee every American private health insurance that can never be taken away, you will force me to take this pen, veto the legislation, and we'll come right back here and start all over again."[4] Some advisers had suggested he take a more moderate approach and seek compromise, but he rejected this view with what they considered unusual vehemence.

White House counselor David Gergen was among those who thought they knew why: Clinton needed to appease Hillary. A series of embarrassing stories had recently surfaced in publications that ranged from the scandal-mongering *American Spectator* to the relatively staid *Los Angeles Times* detailing Clinton's sexual antics

as governor, which included using state police to procure partners. Observing him during that time, Gergen later remembered
of his interactions with Hillary was like watching "a bouncy
golden retriever who has pooped on the living room rug, he just
curled up and looked baleful for days." *Washington Post* reporter
John Harris noted that Gergen was not alone in the view that it
was not politic to question the president's wife's role or the reasons for it. (Gergen, who would soon leave the administration, did
not reveal his opinion publicly until years later.)[5]

The Clinton hard line proved to be a miscalculation. For all
the genuine interest in his plan, and concern among Republicans
that he couldn't be stopped, resistance solidified relatively
quickly. The most obvious and compelling form were the corpo-
rate-financed "Harry and Louise" ads that ran on television,
dramatizing the lives of a middle class couple as they discuss—
with furrowed brows of concern and growing outrage—the al-
legedly heavy-handed details of a Clinton plan that appears to
deny consideration and even care to people like themselves. Opponents also filed a lawsuit over the composition of the task
force, noting that because she was technically not a government
employee (first ladies receive no salary), her participation was illegal. This problem was finessed; but well before the summer of
1994, when Senate Majority Leader George Mitchell officially
announced he could not get the plan through Congress, it was
regarded as dead, never to be revived.[6]

Meanwhile the forces arrayed against Clinton were preparing
to mount a counterrevolution. Ronald Reagan's election to the
presidency in 1980 has rightly been regarded as marking the conservative ascendancy in the United States, but the strength of the
right during and after the Reagan years was far from overpower-
ing. Or, to put it differently, that of a particular Right—the social
conservatives—had always been occluded. Reagan himself paid
far more attention to the Cold War and libertarian economics
(specifically tax cuts) than he did abortion, school prayer, and
other issues dear to this constituency. Many of those who embraced these latter causes felt politically unfulfilled in the 1980s,
and were positively enraged by Bill Clinton, whose feminist wife,
evasion of the draft during the Vietnam War, and libertine

lifestyle—trumpeted by the media during his campaign—person-ified everything they hated about the Baby Boom generation that came of age in the 1960s.

Reagan's successor, George H. W. Bush, had disappointed these people. Getting them back—and filling the power vacuum that emerged in the wake of Bush's defeat—was the goal of the new speaker of the House, Newt Gingrich. Gingrich, a former professor of American history, was elected to Congress in 1978. With a gift for slashing attacks on opponents and compellingly framed conservative perspectives on issues, Gingrich rose through the ranks and successfully led the effort to topple Demo-cratic speaker Jim Wright on charges of corruption. When the moderate House minority leader, Bob Michel, announced his re-tirement, Gingrich put together a legislative program called the "Contract with America" for all House Republicans to run on—and for him to become speaker. The contract consisted of ten items, including term limits, a balanced budget, tougher crime laws, and other provisions, important less for their particulars than for the way it comprised a full and compelling refutation of Clinton. In the midterm elections of 1994, which took place a few months following the failure of the Clinton health care plan, Republicans won a smashing victory, gaining 52 seats in the House as well as 8 in the Senate, giving the GOP a majority in both chambers of Congress for the first time in 40 years. In the aftermath of this crushing defeat, Clinton—not even halfway through his first term—felt compelled to insist that he remained "relevant."

By the beginning of 1995, then, he was well on his way to a historic presidency. But this was not the kind of legacy Clinton had in mind. And years before Monica Lewinsky caught Clin-ton's fancy, his wandering eye was already reaffirming the old feminist adage that the personal truly is political.

"We are ready to go to work, Newt Gingrich wrote in his 1995 manifesto *To Renew America*. "Balancing the budget is the right thing to do."[7]

It may have been the right thing to do, but no presidential administration had been able to do so for over 25 years. Conservative Republicans began making it a centerpiece of their rhetoric during the Reagan years, but were unable to overcome Democratic opposition to cutting various domestic programs—and, in any case, showed time and again that they were far more interested in tax cuts for the wealthy (which they said, arguably, would stimulate the economy as a whole) than reducing overall federal spending. Of course, in and of itself, the federal government spending more than it takes in on any given year is not necessarily a problem—indeed, it would be impossible to embark on some enterprises, like fight wars, without deficit spending. But year after year, such collective living beyond national means was making the overall federal debt truly gargantuan. This was the problem Clinton confronted when he came into office and responded to by making the difficult and unpopular decision to raise taxes.

The Contract with America, written largely by Texas congressman Dick Armey but more widely associated with Gingrich, was the Republican response to the Clinton approach to the economy, among other things. Unveiled in the closing weeks of the 1994 midterm elections—it's unclear to what degree it actually shaped their outcome—the contract outlined the actions that Republicans promised to take if they became the majority party in the House of Representatives. Many of the contract's policy ideas originated at The Heritage Foundation, a presumably nonpartisan but very influential conservative think tank. The document itself consisted of a series of propositions, which, after the election, got translated into ten bills, among them the "Fiscal Responsibility Act"—it was part of the conceit of the contract that proposed bills were labeled as ratified "acts"—which called for a constitutional amendment to balance the budget. Like most of the contract, it did indeed get through the House (the only item that didn't, perhaps unsurprisingly, was a bill requiring term limits), but disappeared into the ether after that, whether because the proposal in question never made it through the more ideologically moderate Senate, was voted down, or was ultimately vetoed by Clinton.

The president, for his part, was actively taking stock in the wake of the Republican surge. On election night, he analyzed results in specific districts, assessing which representatives were hurt by policies like his tax increases in 1993 and the gun control bill he signed the same year. He also received a panoply of advice from those who counseled him to stand fast as well as to adapt, some of it from surprising sources. Clinton's friend Taylor Branch, author of an acclaimed multivolume biography of Martin Luther King, Jr., advised him not to "quibble, cavil, cadge, or complain about the Republican victory." Instead, Branch counseled, he should "graciously salute the new majority, and welcome them to a positive historic view of its meaning."[8]

One clear public manifestation of Clinton's adoption of this view was his 1995 State of the Union Address, in which he famously asserted "the era of big government is over" (adding, in a qualification that was usually lost in the discussion that followed, "we can't go back to a time when our citizens were just left to fend for themselves").[9] In the months that followed, Clinton proposed a series of bite-sized proposals, like advocacy of school uniforms, at the advice of Dick Morris, an old political adviser from his gubernatorial days who Clinton brought back into the fold. Morris, who usually worked for Republicans, repelled many of Clinton's advisers, but his poll-tested propositions, right down to where the Clinton family should vacation, had an oracular quality that the president found compelling.

In one crucial case, Clinton engaged with a major objective of the Contract with America: welfare reform. For decades, Republicans had bemoaned the excesses of government aid to the poor, alternating between complaints that many people abused the system—Reagan's notorious complaints about "welfare queens" who collected benefits and kept having illegitimate children resonated broadly—and concern that welfare actually victimized recipients by engendering a "culture of poverty." By the 1970s even many Democrats, notably New York senator Daniel Patrick Moynihan, were expressing such concerns. One of the major legislative proposals of the Contract with America was the "Personal Responsibility Act," discouraging illegitimacy and teen pregnancy by prohibiting welfare to mothers under 18 years of age, denying increased Aid for Dependent Families with Children (AFDC) benefits for additional children while on welfare, and enacting a two-year limit with work requirements to promote individual responsibility.

Even before he had been thrust on the defensive, Clinton was receptive to the idea of reforming welfare: It was precisely the kind of issue that appealed to his entrepreneurial "New Democrat" side. The difference was that while the Republicans pushed the idea in the hope of fostering discipline-based values for the poor and lighter burdens for taxpayers, Clinton was thinking of improving the quality and efficiency of the system and ensuring his reelection by passing a crowd-pleasing law (not necessarily in that order). Indeed, in the give-and-take that followed during 1995 and most of 1996, Clinton happily irritated stalwart congressional liberals as well as equally stalwart congressional conservatives as part of a Morris-shaped strategy of "triangulation." The revised welfare bill Clinton would finally sign in 1996—after vetoing two previous versions—rounded some of the sharper edges in the Republican plan (the time limits would ultimately be five years, not three, for example) while genuinely outraging some old allies in revising the system so that it became a series of block grants to states. In moving to the center, and honoring his 1995 State of the Union pledge to "end welfare as we know it," he had seized the high ground by parrying the thrusts of his most powerful opponents.[10]

The place were he would engage them in what proved to be a defining battle was over the federal budget for the fiscal year 1996, which was fought over the course of 1995. All year long, Clinton had responded to Republican efforts to slash spending with a mantra-like injunction of the need to protect "Medicaid, Medicare, education and the environment." The sticking point proved to be Medicare and Medicaid: Clinton objected to a reduction in the rate of the increase of federal aid to these programs. Democrats called this a spending cut; Republicans responded by saying this was in fact incorrect and accused the Democrats of demagoguery in frightening senior citizens into thinking that Republicans would endanger their health.

The climax of the struggle came that fall, when the two sides could not come to an agreement. When congressional leaders in-serted a provision raising insurance premiums for Medicare recipients, Clinton decided not to sign a procedural "Continuing Resolution" that allowed government operations to be maintained in the absence of a budget. Without such a resolution, the government would go into default and shut down, because, technically at least, there would be no money. In an effort to prevent such an outcome, a GOP delegation that included Dick Armey, Gingrich, and presidential-hopeful Bob Dole came to the White House on November 13. The government would shut down at midnight. Gingrich and Dole, as it turned out, were inclined to be accommodating. Armey was not. He accused Clinton of terrifying his own mother-in-law over the Medicare "cut." "We could hardly get her into a nursing home, you guys scared her so much," he told the president.[11]

"I don't know about your mother-in-law, but let me tell you there are a lot of older women who are going to do pretty darn bad under your budget," Clinton shot back. The president had his own grievances about Republican scare tactics. They had claimed, falsely, that his tax increases in 1993 would wreck the economy. Armey himself had called Hillary a Marxist during the health care battle. "So don't look for any pity from me."

"If you want to pass your budget, you're going to have to put somebody else in this chair," Clinton continued, looking at Dole. "I don't care what happens. I don't care if I go to five percent in the polls. I am not going to sign your budget. It is wrong. It is wrong for the country."

"This was supposed to be a negotiation," Armey replied. Instead, he complained, he was being forced to "listen to all these lies."

"Mr. Armey, at least I never, ever have and never expect to criticize your wife or any member of your family."[12] The meeting was effectively over.

Clinton aides were elated to learn of the confrontation. Vice President Gore, whose lively sense of humor was rarely evident in public settings, told the president that the whole nation should have witnessed the exchange. "It's very moving to hear that you are willing to lose this election for what you believe in," he said. "Just one little thing: When you said you don't care if your popularity goes down to five percent, I think it would sound a little better if you said, 'I don't care if my popularity goes down to zero.'"

Clinton, whose wit was not generally as sharp, wrapped his arm around Gore. "No, that's not right, Al," he replied. "If I go down to four percent I'm caving." The room erupted in laughter.[13]

Hours later, the shutdown of the federal government became official. The doors of all offices not deemed essential remained shut; all employees deemed non-essential stayed home. National governmental operations of everything from national parks to the National Weather Service were suspended. Far from worrying about this, however, Clinton made the most of the shutdown. He ordered his cabinet secretaries to compile lists of popular functions that were not operating, which he recited at public appearances over the course of the coming days. People complained about the federal government all the time, he realized. But in the end, they wanted it there to meet their needs. And if it wasn't there, he strongly suspected he wasn't going to be the one voters blamed.

He was right. Gingrich, for his part, overplayed his hand with an incidental remark that hurt him badly. The previous week, he had been part of an American delegation that accompanied Clinton to the funeral of Yitzhak Rabin, the Israeli prime minister who had been assassinated. Upon his return, Gingrich was informed that he should get off Air Force One at the back of the plane with the White House staff and press corps. At a November 15 breakfast meeting, he complained about it. "You land at Andrews Air Force base and you've been on the plane for 25 hours and nobody has talked to you and they ask you to get off the plane at the back ramp," he reported. "It's petty. But it's human."[14]

Yet the effect of these remarks was to make Gingrich look petty and human in the most unattractive of ways. "CRY BABY," blared the headline of the New York *Daily News*—no friend to Clinton. In fact, the decision to hold Gingrich at arm's length was intentional, though not on Clinton's part. Chief of Staff Leon Panetta and presidential aide George Stephanopoulos had been afraid that Clinton would be tempted to cut a budget deal with Gingrich and Dole and so orchestrated their separation. But the president did his part by exploiting Gingrich's churlishness with an extravagant display of magnanimity. "I can tell you this," he said in reaction to the furor. "If it would get the government open, I would be glad to tell him I'm sorry."[15]

In truth, though, the shutdown was fraying nerves and even alliances. By Sunday, November 19, six days into the crisis, 48 Democrats had voted for a new Continuing Resolution (CR) that did not have the Medicare premium increase but did demand the budget be balanced in seven years. Actually, balancing the budget was something Clinton himself was on the record supporting, so he decided to go along with signing a new CR. The Republicans then passed a budget—and Clinton vetoed it. By this point, it was mid-December; Gingrich and Dole realized that another shutdown, particularly in holiday season, could only hurt their image. Democrats held together; Republicans capitulated.

Clinton had won an important victory. In so doing, he demonstrated the kind of political resilience that made his newfound relevance all the more impressive. It led to a surprisingly easy reelection campaign in 1996 against the admirable but hapless Dole. There was another budget showdown at the end of that year, but Treasury Secretary Robert Rubin was able to use accounting legerdemain to insulate the public from a second, but effectively technical, shutdown in December 1996–January 1997.

By that point, Clinton was looking ahead to a term of smooth sailing. As it turned out, however, the government shutdown would have another important consequence that would greatly complicate his second term. The furlough of federal workers in November 1995 meant there was plenty of slack to be picked up even at the White House. And one person eager to pick it up, and who had caught Clinton's eye, was the young unpaid intern Monica Lewinsky. She was pulled from her job working for Panetta in the Old Executive Office Building and put to work answering phones in the West Wing. It was all downhill from there.

Few presidents came into office with as full and complex understanding of the presidency as Bill Clinton. More than that: Few presidents came into office with as potent a sense of ambition as Bill Clinton. He came, as his boosters never tired of repeating, from a place called Hope, and the arc of his life—modest, even abusive beginnings in an awkwardly blended family; a fierce intellect propelling him through Georgetown and Yale; a volatile but highly synergetic partnership with a comparably ambitious wife; early success as the "boy governor," followed by defeat and decisive recovery—was widely considered eloquent testimony to the ongoing validity of American Dream mythology. Clinton had an intense sense of history as well as destiny, and as good a preparation for the office as any of his peers. Lyndon Johnson wanted to out-Roosevelt Roosevelt. Clinton's ambition was not quite to out-Johnson Johnson—his childhood idol was Johnson's John F. Kennedy, whom he met on a school trip in 1963—but he did want to tackle big social problems in American life in a way that no president had since the time of the Great Society. The signature issue he chose to make his mark was health care reform. But that particular chapter of his career had a decisively unhappy ending, and one that haunts us to this day, as the number, and proportion, of uninsured Americans continues to grow.

It seems highly unlikely Bill Clinton will ever be viewed as a great president. He suffered the humiliation of being only the second chief executive in American history to be impeached (putting him in the company of another Southern Democrat, the inauspicious Andrew Johnson), and while it was obvious at the time that Clinton's opponents were hardly paragons of fair-mindedness, his own self-indulgent behavior provided the indispensable fuel for their fire. Health care reform was the only bold undertaking of his presidency, and it failed. Of course, that put him in good company, since FDR, Truman, and even Johnson had failed to make much headway in the way Clinton wanted to, and all three of those presidents had a much more promising ideological and partisan climate than Clinton ever did.

Actually, it was that climate above all else that circumscribed him. Lacking a war, depression—or, for that matter, the rising public confidence TR and LBJ could exploit—Clinton simply lacked the opportunity to change the political hand he was dealt. An ambivalent liberal in a conservative age, he operated most effectively when reacting to the initiatives of others rather than blazing his own trail.

One should not underestimate, however, the impact that a reactive response can nevertheless have. By the start of the twenty-first century, the American right had pretty much reached a point that the American left had thirty years before: excess. In their very different ways, both had become mindlessly ideological and outrageously self-indulgent. And in an ironic way, Clinton's presidency finds its parallel in Nixon's, not only in the intensity of the hatred the two men generated—though it really must be repeated that Clinton's offenses pale by comparison—but in the way their wiliness confounded those who wanted to take the country in a very different direction.

There is one other thing Clinton and Nixon have in common that seems worth noting as we come to the close of this narrative: They're the only two presidents in the second half of the twentieth century to enjoy balanced budgets. Nixon came into office with one in 1969,[16] and Clinton went out with one in 2001, doing so ahead of the schedule he pledged with the Republicans in 1995, and generating a surplus for the fiscal year in 1998 and for the next four years in a row. By the time he left office, the once terrifying national debt was shrinking rapidly. Of course, a great deal of the credit for this accomplishment is attributable to the surging American economy of the 1990s, and despite the credit and blame presidents get for economic conditions, they are something over which chief executives have limited control at best. Still, there is little in the record of Republican presidents before and after Clinton, whatever the economic circumstances, to lead one to conclude they had comparable seriousness about the government living within its means. When it came to what had presumably been the hallmark of conservative budget ideology since the 1960s, Clinton proved to be a model Republican.

This achievement has not proven durable, however. From the vantage point of a mere half-dozen years later, it almost seems like a mirage that one of the most contested issues in the election of 2000 was what should be done with the federal budget surplus. Tax cuts, increased federal spending (in yet one more irony, it was a Republican who implemented the first major expansion in national health care, with the prescription drug enhancement of Medicare), and a financially ruinous war whose costs the American people have not yet begun to absorb have more than wiped out anything Clinton was able to do by way of fiscal discipline. This story ends at the start of the twenty-first century where it began at the end of the eighteenth: with a nation at war, in financial distress, and far more vulnerable than most of its citizens realize.

# PRESIDENT BUSH FUMBLES AN INVASION

*In which we see why this book was written*

And the current occupant of the White House? What about him?

It's a fair question. Historians often try to sidestep contemporary events and avoid forecasting legacies, pointing out that historical hindsight tends to be better than predictive foresight and invoking the pitfalls of failing to respect "the pastness of the past." The classic example of a misapplied lesson is that of Cold War American policymakers; they used a "Munich" analogy—alluding to European appeasement in the face of Nazi aggression at a 1938 peace conference—to argue that they had to avoid repeating such a mistake by containing aggressive Communists around the world. The result was the quagmire of Vietnam (and some lesser-known debacles).[1] But unless we feel that the study of the past has *some* relevance for the present, history becomes pointless. "It is no argument against the use of analogy to say it is dangerous," the great American historian C. Vann Woodward wrote toward the end of his long life. "So is the historian's use of evidence, comparison, or, for that matter, metaphor. . . History is a perilous craft."[2] And, for all the perils, an essential one. The writer of a history of the American presidency may be tempted to avoid a discussion of the sitting president and hazarding a guess as to his future reputation, but the failure to do so would be both disappointing and maybe even dishonest.

The task of assessing President George W. Bush carries with it an additional difficulty, one more pronounced in his case than in that of many of his contemporaries: Mr. Bush is a man who generates strong and polarized feelings. The historian who forgets that there are many intelligent and principled people who disagree with him is one virtually begging to be rejected or—worse still—ignored.

There are, in fact, any number of ways in which President Bush can be usefully compared with his predecessors. As we all know, he comes from a notably privileged background, as have many presidents, notably the two Roosevelts. He is the son of a president, as was John Quincy Adams. And like these people and many others, George W. Bush surmounted significant personal challenges, in his case, a struggle with alcoholism (one overcome, as is often the case with such challenges, with the love of a good woman). Like many of these people as well, Mr. Bush is often cited as having an impressive common touch; his oft-cited verbal gaffes have been at least as likely to charm as offend voters, in part because he has a becoming modesty in this regard that allows him to be seen as an approachable, likable man. The same could be said for his religious faith, which he typically inhabits with unselfconscious sincerity. These are traits he shares with many previous presidents, and traits that are legitimately cherished as positive reasons why such a person should be the choice of American voters.

Indeed, while the president's critics often point to a paucity of achievements in his public life—derided as a failed oil man guilty of dubious financial manipulation as his company collapsed—the fact is that the man's electoral success is an achievement in its own right. While there are real reasons to suspect the legitimacy of both the 2000 and 2004 presidential elections in Florida and Ohio, respectively, Bush never could have prevailed in these contests (not to mention the governorship of Texas) without significant electoral support of about half the electorate in those states and nationally, support that rested on an ability to win the confidence of voters as well as attract the talent of campaign professionals who chose to invest their talents in him rather than his competitors. Presidential candidates, even rich presidential candidates with burnished backgrounds, are a dime a dozen. It's not possible to elect an empty suit President of the United States, notwithstanding periodic satires asserting otherwise.

All that said, this book was written in the belief that George W. Bush has been a disastrously bad president—among the worst the United States has ever had. This would not appear to be a particularly good venue to either preach to the converted or persuade skeptics—there are plenty of books devoted entirely to those enterprises—though it does appear necessary to briefly explain why for now, at least, there is no triumph here to pair with the misadventures of the Bush administration.

The defining moment of the Bush presidency occurred with the terrorist attacks of September 11, 2001. Many Americans—even those who did not vote for him—believe that Bush responded to that crisis with forceful resolve. (They thought so even as they subsequently learned from an investigatory commission, whose creation the administration resisted, that the government ignored repeated warnings—among other occasions a presidential briefing weeks before the attacks—that the terrorist threat was growing.) The first move the administration made was to strike back at the Taliban regime in Afghanistan, which harbored the camps of Al Qaeda leader Osama bin Laden. While the Taliban was indeed quickly toppled—though Osama bin Laden remains at large as of this writing—that struggle is ongoing. The United States, like the Soviet Union and Great Britain before it, is learning about the challenges of central Asian insurgencies the hard way.

The other, more controversial move the administration made in the aftermath of September 11 was the 2003 invasion of Iraq. While the administration came into office with such a plan, the terrorist attacks gave the idea new energy and legitimacy. Though the regime of Saddam Hussein had no direct connection with those terrorist attacks—something Bush and other officials in his administration admitted when pressed—the invasion was repeatedly cast in terms of the War on Terror, coupled with assertions that the regime of Saddam Hussein was actively engaged in developing weapons of mass destruction (WMD). This turned out to be untrue. Certainly the Bush administration was not alone in believing that Saddam Hussein had such weapons. But it alone chose to wage a war of choice to overthrow his regime, something the president's father chose not to do when he was president.

In part, the first president Bush chose not do so because he feared that centrifugal forces would tear Iraq apart, generating regional instability that would be difficult to contain. While his son could argue that the circumstances had changed in ways that now required him to finish the job, he could not claim that he was unaware of the risks—he was repeatedly warned, by a variety of sources in his own government, of just this possibility. Even if one assumes that the invasion of Iraq was entirely justified and necessary, it seems virtually impossible to assert that it could not have been done in a more efficient and humane manner that did not result in tens of thousands of casualties, American as well as Iraqi. This is particularly true in light of well-documented abuses at the Abu-Gharib prison and the detention camp at Guantanamo Bay—a camp whose legality under domestic and international law was rejected by the Supreme Court. The damage these and other abuses of power have done to the reputation of the United States in the rest of the world has been severe and lasting, even among close allies.[3]

All of the above assertions remain true even if one assumes that the outcome in Iraq will be an independent, democratic, and secure state. But, of course, this is not an assumption that can be confidently made, particularly in light of premature invocations of "mission accomplished," continuing resistance in Iraq, and a growing avalanche of documentation that the Bush administration ignored advice it did not wish to hear before, during, and after the invasion.

One could make similar arguments about the most important event in domestic affairs during Bush's presidency: Hurricane Katrina in 2005.[4] Failure is rarely an orphan, and there is plenty of blame to go around for this catastrophe, inside and outside local, state, and federal government. But it would be impossible for the Bush administration or anyone else to claim that this disaster was unforeseeable, and as with the Iraq war, urgent voices on the eve of the event were ignored at the highest levels. As with the Iraq war, too, there were widespread accusations of incompetence during and after the event. Yet what is finally most haunting both about Iraq and Katrina is not a sense that people in charge didn't know what they were doing, but rather that they did—both events occurred against a backdrop of what appeared to be a systematic downgrading of government resources and capacity, and a systematic emphasis on private interests, whether in awarding contracts to corporate firms or bringing the heads of such firms in to run the government. This emphasis on the private gain at the expense of the public good seemed especially evident in the principal domestic initiative of the Bush administration, the Medicare drug plan.

The Medicare drug plan, in turn, raises questions about the president's core principles. Many small-government conservatives found themselves wondering just how the vast expansion of the federal government on Bush's watch—a term that, in the aftermath of increased surveillance efforts after 9/11, can be taken literally—could be called conservative at all. Ditto for the highly centralized "No Child Left Behind" Act of 2001, which mandated test-driven standards for education performance without resources to match—or much scrutiny about the quality of those standards. Fiscal conservatives watched in amazement as Bush declined to veto a single spending bill (though he did make clear, over 100 times, that he intended to ignore laws he didn't like with so-called signing statements). Social conservatives in particular were outraged about the administration's failure to control immigration—though this, too, raised suspicions that Bush's primary interest, whatever his sincere compassion for Latinos seeking a piece of the American Dream, was the cheap labor they represented to business interests.

Above all, there was government debt—towering, uncounted government debt (costs for the Iraq war and the War on Terror were treated as emergency appropriations not included as items in the regular annual federal budget). Here again, this was a problem that long preceded the Bush administration; indeed, it was one of the factors in his father's defeat in 1992. But the tax cuts that were the centerpiece of Bush II domestic policy—tax cuts that were preserved and expanded in wartime, and tax cuts that disproportionately aided the wealthy at a time when benefits for the working poor, veterans among them, were regularly cut— may well prove to be the single most damaging legacy of the Bush years. When coupled with the vast enlargement in military and homeland security spending, the financial recklessness of the Bush administration amounts to a self-inflicted wound that could conceivably be fatal.[5]

Indeed, one need not be a Bush opponent to be deeply worried about the nation's course in the first decade of the twenty-first century. The challenges the nation faces—among them Asian rivals whose economic power may finally prove far more threatening than the threat from terrorists—daunt patriots of all stripes, whose anxieties could plausibly give way to passive despair. Such views might well prove to be unfounded; many who hold them sincerely hope they're wrong. Few Americans who lived through the height of the Cold War, after all, would have wagered that it would have ended as happily as it did. But worry for the future of our children is hardly an irrational concern.

Among the legacies, cheerfully accepted or not, that may be attributed to the Bush administration is this little book. Written in a time of growing geopolitical turmoil, for a rising generation whose parents inherited a deep sense of skepticism about established authority, it seeks to find, amid abundant evidence of failure, sources of hope—the only real reason to write history. Children today are taught that their parents were taught American leaders were wise and good and embodied what was best about their unsullied country. They know better: The George Washington who chopped down the cherry tree and redeemed himself has been replaced by George Washington the irredeemable slaveholder. The truth, of course, is more complicated.[6] This book has been an effort to discover some of that truth, and render it as simply as possible as part of an effort to find discrete, tempered, but finally legitimate sources of inspiration, sources that may yet steel the better angels of our natures.

The focus of that effort here has been an inquiry into the American presidency—an institution whose symbolic dimensions may well be more important than its constitutional function. And yet at the end of this inquiry, the reality that finally seems most decisive is neither the individual nor the office. We will never understand the Bush presidency simply by looking at George Bush. The reality is bigger, more complex, and finally more elusive than that.

# THE PRESIDENT WE NEED

ost of us, most of the time, don't get the president we want. To some extent, that's because one party controls the presidency about half the time (assuming, dubiously, that most of us have a strong party affiliation). Yet even within the parties, candidates stake out positions along an ideological spectrum, and the candidate who gets chosen almost always represents a shifting and uncertain perception of what constitutes the center. Sometimes we ourselves are near that perceived center; sometimes we're not.

Every once in a while, though—generally once or twice in a lifetime—we get a president that we really like, a president we believe makes a positive difference. Presidents often say they represent all Americans, that the presidency is the only governmental office chosen by the electorate at large, but these landmark presidents are actually believed when they say they represent the people as a whole and not "special interests" (though the concept of what makes an interest "special" can be infuriatingly subjective). They bend the rules, but we ultimately don't mind because we believe their intentions are good. Or, at any rate, that the results are good.

Indeed, it's difficult to escape the conclusion that virtually all presidents, good and bad alike, do not simply have foibles but actually break laws. Andrew Jackson's treatment of the Cherokees, Abraham Lincoln's suspension of the writ of habeas corpus, George W. Bush's designation of "enemy combatants" without rights in the War on Terror: In hindsight, these acts are difficult, even impossible, to justify. And these were considered decisions made by presidents with at least some public support. The same could not be said of Lyndon Johnson's electoral tactics in the Senate election of 1948, Richard Nixon's actions in the aftermath of the Watergate break-in, or Bill Clinton's tactics in pursuing sexual gratification before and during his presidency.

Legal rectitude is simultaneously too limited—and too high—a standard by which to judge presidents. "The law will never make men free; it is men who have got to make the law free," Henry David Thoreau once wrote.[1] Thoreau was referring to his outrage that an escaped slave in Massachusetts was being returned to his owner in accord with the evil Fugitive Slave Act of 1850. But his remark is thoroughly apposite when one considers the varied situations of George Washington refusing to become a dictator, John Quincy Adams refusing to abide the Gag Rule, and Chester Alan Arthur signing the Pendleton Act. All of these people had to bend, break, or make rules in ways that ignored history or interest and affirmed a higher law—an affirmation fraught with danger, to be sure, but whose refusal to contemplate is at least as dangerous. Thoreau's remark is also profound despite the powerful impression one has of him as an irascible misanthrope who could be both impractical as well as hypocritical (no one who leaves the woods to have his mother do his laundry is self-reliant).[2]

So private character isn't a perfect tape measure, either. You might not want Thomas Jefferson as your friend, but he was an undeniably inspiring politician. Conversely, many of the current President Bush's policies have been disastrous even as anecdotes proliferate of him being an unusually personable man. Clearly, character counts; all of the men here have flaws, but even many of those flaws are merely flipsides of real virtues.

A better measure of presidential ability may be an individual's capacity to embody the dominant strains—"strains" as in characteristics, as well as tensions or even contradictions—of a time. Theodore Roosevelt addressed a desire for a critical assessment and reform of public as well as private institutions in American life. Ronald Reagan, for his part, addressed a yearning in the American public for a return to tradition and an assertion of national optimism. Giving the people what they desire—and the not-inconsiderable matter of being able to figure out what they desire in the first place—is surely an important component in becoming the president the people want.

Yet it may be that the most important thing a president can do is not give us what we want, but to motivate us to accept or do something valuable that we were unaware of wanting—or perhaps actively did not want at all. Many Americans were deeply skeptical at the prospect of ending slavery, fighting World War II, or forgiving Richard Nixon, but the presidents who executed these policies relied less on force than on compelling and persuasive arguments that sooner or later brought most fellow citizens around to their point of view. In short, they offered leadership.

Of course, leadership can be a slippery thing. What one person considers leadership another might consider coercion, and no president can succeed on leadership alone: Effective governance is a two-way street. Listening and compliance as well are essential ingredients. No one understood this better than Abraham Lincoln. "With public sentiment, nothing can fail; without it, nothing can succeed," he said during his first debate with Stephen Douglas in 1858. "Consequently, he who moulds public sentiment goes deeper than he who enacts statutes or pronounces decisions." Great presidents lead, and leading well involves understanding who it is you're leading. And that involves paying close attention—something an isolated president may find difficult to do.

In the end though, we really must go back to the beginning. On a day-to-day basis, the governmental machinery of the United States proceeds on its own. It doesn't finally matter who the president is. What matters is who the people are: What presidential behavior they will accept, which presidential decisions they will support, how presidential acts will affect their hearts and minds. Those fascinated by the workings of the American government, and those who feel hostile or powerless toward it, may make the same mistake of attributing too much significance to the presumed person in charge. Here too Thoreau's remark is apt (and more in keeping with the point he was trying to make): It is men and women collectively, not heroic individuals, who make the law free. In a functioning democracy, the president we need is a president we don't need. That's what George Washington showed us—that's the gift George Washington gave us—in Newburgh, New York, on the Ides of March, 1783. Because of what Washington did not do, Caesar was not resurrected, and a republic was born.

# READING GUIDE

*Foreword: The President We Want*
This book considers the careers of a dozen presidents, from George Washington to George W. Bush. There are dozens more it does not consider, and no presidents Cullen discusses served consecutively. Which presidents might you have included in this volume? Which misadventures would you choose, and which triumphs might you pair with them? (Some suggestions: Andrew Jackson and Cherokee removal or nullification; John F. Kennedy and the Bay of Pigs or the nuclear test ban treaty; Jimmy Carter and the Iranian crisis or in his post-presidential career.)

*Prologue: George Washington Coddles a Protégé*
How would you describe the tone of the Washington-Hamilton conversation as it emerges in their correspondence? How does Hamilton address Washington? How would you describe Washington's stance toward Hamilton?

*Chapter 1: Vice-President Jefferson Stabs a Friend in the Back*
Considered as a matter of politics—as opposed to one of friendship or statesmanship—how do you regard James Madison's advice that Thomas Jefferson spurn the advances of President-Elect John Adams? To what degree *can* the politics of the matter be separated from friendship or statesmanship?

*Chapter 2: Former President Adams Can't Stop Gagging*
JQ was opposed to slavery his whole life, but his opposition did not become energetic and public until the end of his life, and he had relatively little contact with slaves at any point in his life.

Indeed, some, among them Adams himself, would hesitate to even consider him an abolitionist. What do you think motivated Adams in the gag rule fight? Was it principle? Irritation with Southerners and/or the people who opposed him? A difficult personality?

### Chapter 3: Representative Lincoln Smears a Preacher

"Men are not flattered by being shown there has been a difference between the Almighty and them," Lincoln said of his Second Inaugural Address. "To deny it, however, in this case, is to deny there is a God governing the world. It is a truth that I thought needed to be told; and as whatever of humiliation there is in it, falls most directly on myself, I thought others might afford for me to tell it." (p. 71) What "humiliation" do you think Lincoln refers to here? Do you believe he's right to shoulder such blame?

### Chapter 4: "Gentleman Boss" Arthur Bites the Hand that Feeds Him

Chester Alan Arthur defied his mentor Roscoe Conkling to accept the vice-presidency in 1880, and again in his policies after he became president. This proved to be politically wise; was it morally wrong? (Be sure to factor Conkling's own conduct in your answer.)

### Chapter 5: Dude T.R. Enters the Arena

"Great corporations exist only because they are created and safeguarded by our institutions; and it is therefore our right and our duty to see that they work in harmony with these institutions," TR said in his first State of the Union Address in 1901 (p. 95). Is this statement relevant today? If so, how would you apply it?

### Chapter 6: F.D.R. Courts Disaster

"In important respects, this is still Roosevelt's world," Cullen writes in the conclusion of this chapter. "We just live in it. In the half-life of its afterglow, we're damned lucky" (p. 115). What do you think he means by this? Why *damned* lucky? Do you agree?

## Chapter 7: "Landslide Lyndon" Takes a Position

"I left the woman I really loved – the Great Society – in order to get involved with that bitch on the other side of the world," LBJ famously said (p132). Do you regard the unhappy ending of Johnson's presidency as a tragedy, as a matter of just desserts, or some other way?

## Chapter 8: Vice-President Ford Stumbles at the Gate

"It is not the ultimate fate of Richard Nixon that most concerns me, though it surely troubles every decent and compassionate person," Ford said of his pardon of the former president. "My concern is the immediate concern of this great country." (p. 142) Do you believe Ford? Whether or not you do, was pardoning Nixon the nation's interest in the short term? How about the long term?

## Chapter Nine: "The Gipper" Loses One

"That was the thing about Reagan," Cullen writes at the end of this chapter. "Even when you disagreed with him – even when you knew in your heart he was wrong – the man was irresistible." (The phrase "in your heart you know he's right" was a campaign slogan for the 1964 Republican presidential candidate Barry Goldwater, who Reagan supported.) In what sense would you – or wouldn't you – say Reagan was "irresistible"?

## Chapter 10: "Slick Willie" Slips and Falls

Cullen believes that Clinton's success as president was less a matter of what he did than what he prevented, i.e., the set of policies known as the "Contract with America" advanced by Newt Gingrich and other conservative Republicans in the 1994 midterm elections. Can a president ever be considered great on such terms? Can you offer an example of someone who was?

## Epilogue: President Bush Fumbles and Invasion:

"We will never understand the Bush presidency simply by looking at George Bush," Cullen writes. (p. 191) One implication of this remark is that individual Americans bear some responsibility for how things have turned out. How much blame are you willing to accept? If you didn't vote for him, do you bear any?

### *Afterword: The President We Need*
Cullen quotes Abraham Lincoln as saying, "With public sentiment nothing can fail; without it, nothing can succeed." (p. 195) How important is public opinion to the success of a presidency today? How long, and in what ways, can a president proceed without it?

# NOTES

## PROLOGUE

1. Alexander Hamilton to George Washington, February 13, 1783, in Alexander Hamilton, *Writings*, edited by Joanne B. Freeman (New York: Library of America, 2001), 122.
2. George Washington to Alexander Hamilton, March 4, 1783, in George Washington, *Writings*, edited by John Rhodehamel (New York: Library of America, 1997), 489.
3. George Washington to Continental Congress, September 24, 1776, Washington Papers at the Library of Congress: http://lcweb2.loc.gov.
4. Thomas Paine, *The Crisis*, December 23, 1776, http://www.ushistory.org/Paine/crisis/c-01.htm.
5. James Thomas Flexner, *George Washington in the Revolution, 1775–1783* (Boston: Little, Brown, 1968), 503–504; Lewis Nicola to George Washington, May 22, 1782 in Washington, *Writings*, 1106; Washington to Nicola, May 22, 1782 in Washington, *Writings*, 468–469.
6. Washington to Joseph Jones, December 14, 1782, in Washington, *Writings*, 479; Flexner, *George Washington in the Revolution*, 501.
7. The petition is cited in Richard Kohn, "The Inside History of the Newburgh Conspiracy: America and the Coup d'Etat," *William and Mary Quarterly* 27:2 (April 1970), 189.
8. Kohn, 194–195.
9. Kohn, 206–207.
10. Washington, "General Orders," March 11, 1783, in Washington, *Writings*, 490.
11. Kohn, 208–209.
12. Washington to Hamilton, March 12, 1783, in Washington, *Writings*, 491–492.

13.   Washington, "Speech to the Officers of the Army," in Washington, *Writings*, 496–499.
14.   Kohn, 210.
15.   Kohn, 211.
16.   George III quoted in Gordon S. Wood, "The Greatness of George Washington," in *Revolutionary Characters: What Made the Founders Different* (New York: The Penguin Press, 2006), 42.

## CHAPTER ONE

1.   "My friends inform me that Mr. A. speaks of me with great friendship and with satisfaction of administering the government in concurrence with me," Jefferson noted in early 1797. For this and more on the origins of the Adams-Jefferson rift, see Joseph J. Ellis, *Founding Brothers: The Revolutionary Generation* (New York: Vintage, 2002), 179.
2.   The immediate cause of the rift between the two friends was Adams's 1790 publication of *Discourses on Davila*, a tract controversial for Adams's support of a monarchy and aristocracy in countries such as France, and his denunciation of equality based on his belief that humans naturally have "a passion for distinction." Jefferson, who did not share Adams's skepticism about the French Revolution or the power of reason, did not reply directly, but the following year warmly endorsed Thomas Paine's prorevolutionary tract *The Rights of Man*, a reply to the English conservative Edmund Burke. In a note that Jefferson included when forwarding his copy to a printer for an American edition—a note he claimed was mistakenly published as part of that edition—Jefferson pointedly decried "political heresies that have sprung up among us." This remark was widely understood to be a swipe at Adams. Jefferson tried to paper over the differences with an apology, but a durable chill had set in. That chill deepened when a 1796 letter to an Italian friend was published abroad without his knowledge decrying "men who were Solomons in council, and Samsons in combat, but whose hair has been cut off by the whore England," leaving little doubt of his biblical allusions to Adams and Washington respectively. See Ellis, *Founding Brothers*, 168–169.
3.   American politicians had not yet grasped the implications of having an executive branch headed by people who were ideological opponents. The Founding Fathers found the idea of political par-

tisanship unseemly at best and dangerously divisive at worst, and made no formal allowances for it. In the aftermath of the election of 1796—and the even more problematic election of 1800, which created a dangerous political deadlock between Jefferson and his unfriendly ally, Aaron Burr—the government ratified the Twelfth Amendment to the Constitution (1804), which created a ticket of presumably like-minded candidates for president and vice president on a single slate. Frictions between the two positions did subsequently surface from time to time (see, for example, Franklin Roosevelt's relationship with John Nance Garner in chapter seven), but not to the same degree.

4. David McCulloch, *John Adams* (New York: Simon & Schuster, 2001), 465–466; Thomas Jefferson to James Madison, January 1, 1797, in *Basic Writings of Thomas Jefferson* (New York: Wiley, 1944), 634–635; Jefferson to Edward Rutledge, December 27, 1796, www.cooperativeindividualism.org/jefferson_r_02.html.

5. Jefferson to Adams, December 28, 1796, in *Basic Writings of Thomas Jefferson*, 633–634.

6. James Madison to Thomas Jefferson, January 15, 1797, http://www.constitution.org/jm/17970115_tj.htm.

7. Ellis, *Founding Brothers*, 183.

8. Adams's wife Abigail, a political confidant who had endorsed the rapprochement with Jefferson, was aware it was not working out as early as January 15. "The cold has been more severe than I can ever before recollect," she wrote of her pained perception that Jefferson had spurned them. "It has frozen the ink in my pen, and chilled the blood in my veins, but not the warmth of my affection for him for whom my heart beats through all the vicissitudes of life." See McCulloch, *John Adams*, 466.

9. James Madison to Nicholas P. Trist, May, 1832, http://www.constitution.org/jm/18320500_trist.txt.

10. Jefferson's letter can be accessed at the Yale Law School's Avalon Project: http://www.yale.edu/lawweb/avalon/presiden/inaug/jefinau1.htm.

11. See the University of Virginia's Thomas Jefferson Digital Archive: http://etext.virginia.edu/jefferson/biog/lj23.htm.

12. Jefferson quoted in Thomas Fleming, *The Louisiana Purchase* (Hoboken, NJ: John Wiley & Sons), 4.

13. Talleyrand, who served every French ruler for a half century that stretched from Louis XVI in the 1780s to Louis Philippe in the 1830s, fell from favor briefly in the mid-1790s and took asylum in

the United States. The experience engendered not gratitude but contempt for Americans, whom he regarded as crude and callow. His ministry helped trigger the Quasi War by demanding a bribe from the unnamed American delegation, an event known to students of American history as the XYZ Affair. And he continued his machinations after it was over.

14. Tallyrand quoted in Fleming, 6.

15. The four cents per acre figure is widely cited. See, for example, the Louisiana Purchase Legislative timeline at the Library of Congress American Memory website: http://memory.loc.gov /ammem/amlaw/louisianapurchase.html.

16. Jefferson to Wilson Cary Nicholas, September 7, 1803, http://grid.let.rug.nl/usa.990917/P/tj3/writings/brf/jefl160.htm.

17. Joseph J. Ellis, *American Sphinx: The Character of Thomas Jefferson* (1996; New York: Vintage, 1998), 252.

## CHAPTER TWO

1. *The Diary of John Quincy Adams, 1795–1845*, edited by Allan Nevins (New York: Longmans, Greens & Co., 1929), 157 (Feb. 7, 1815).

2. *Diary of JQA* (May 8, 1824), 322–23.

3. Robert V. Remini, *John Quincy Adams* (New York: Times Books, 2002), 79–85. Adams was one of the principal figures, amid much Congressional opposition, who steered the $500,000 bequest of James Smithson into the founding of a national museum: The Smithsonian Institution.

4. *Diary of JQA* (Feb. 24, 1820), 228–229.

5. Adams quoted in William Lee Miller, *Arguing About Slavery: John Quincy Adams and the Great Battle in the United States Congress* (1995; New York: Vintage Books, 1998), 198.

6. Miller, 206–209.

7. Miller, 225–230.

8. Miller, 230–237.

9. Miller, 349; 364–365.

10. Miller, 318.

11. Miller, 423.

12. Much of the subsequent account draws heavily, though not exclusively, from Miller, 430–444. It's worth noting the irony here that the outrage is being expressed by South Carolinians, as South

Carolina would ultimately be the first state to leave the Union in 1861.

13. *Diary of JQA* (March 29, 1841), 519.
14. *Diary of JQA* (Feb. 11, 1820), 226.

## CHAPTER THREE

1. One may wonder, given that it was not written in his name, how one can be sure of the authorship of the piece in question. In fact, this has not yet been scientifically documented (though the computer analysis of prose patterns is an emerging tool of authentication that may yet do so beyond any doubt). There are, however, multiple sources corroborating Lincoln's authorship of this letter. See Douglas Wilson, *Honor's Voice: The Transformation of Abraham Lincoln* (New York: Vintage, 1998), 298–301. We do know, in any event, that in at least one case, Lincoln would own up to having penned such anonymous attacks (the so-called Rebecca Letters), when one of the subjects of his ridicule challenged him to a duel, resulting in a tense and embarrassing standoff that was averted only at the last minute.

2. Abraham Lincoln, "Handbill Replying to Charges of Infidelity," in *Lincoln: Speeches, Letters, and Miscellaneous Writings 1832–1858*, edited by Don Fehrenbacher (New York: Library of America, 1989), 139–140.

3. The exchange is quoted in Wilson, 83.

4. Lincoln to John D. Johnston, January 12, 1851, in *Speeches and Writings 1832–1858*, 256.

5. Lincoln, to Joshua Speed, August 24, 1855, in *Speeches and Writings 1832–1858*, 360–361.

6. Lincoln and Dan Stone, "Protest in the Illinois Legislature on Slavery," in *Speeches and Writings 1832–1858*, 18.

7. Lincoln's Reply, Seventh Debate with Stephen A. Douglas, Alton, Illinois, October 15, 1858, in *Speeches and Writings 1832–1858*, 807.

8. Lincoln, "Farewell Address at Springfield Illinois," February 11, 1861, in *Abraham Lincoln: Speeches, Letters and Miscellaneous Writings, 1859–1865*, edited by Don Fehrenbacher (New York: Library of America, 1989), 199.

9. Lincoln, circa early September 1862, "Meditation on the Divine Will"; Lincoln, "Response to Serenade," September 24, 1862, in *Speeches and Writings 1859–1865*, 359, 372.

10. Lincoln to Albert G. Hodges, April 4, 1864, in *Speeches and Writings 1859–1865*, 586.

11. Herndon quoted in Allen C. Guelzo, *Abraham Lincoln: Redeemer President* (1999; Grand Rapids, MI: William B. Erdmans, 2003), 120. Guelzo's discussion of Lincoln's religiosity is among the most nuanced in print.

12. Lincoln, "On Pro-Slavery Theology," *Speeches and Writings 1832–1859*, 685.

13. Lincoln, Second Inaugural Address, March 4, 1865, in *Speeches and Writings 1859–1865*.

14. Lincoln to Thurlow Weed, March 15, 1865, *Speeches and Writings, 1832–1859*, 689.

15. Richard Hofstadter, *The American Political Tradition* (1948; New York: Vintage, 1959), 135.

## CHAPTER FOUR

1. This and the ensuing lines of dialogue, a fixture of the discourse on Arthur, were first reported by journalist William Hudson almost thirty years after the fact, and may thus be apocryphal. But they certainly reflect the consensus about what happened at the 1880 convention. The most readily available contemporary account of their exchange can be found in Zachary Karabell, *Chester Alan Arthur* (New York: Times Books, 2004), 41–42.

2. Stalwarts represented what was then considered the conservative wing of the Republican party, which meant, among other things, a strong stand in favor of civil rights for African Americans along with an avowed embrace of party-building activities that even in this lax time were widely considered corrupt. Their opponents, the Half-Breeds, were known for their willingness to cooperate with Democrats on matters like ending Reconstruction in the South and advocating Civil Service reforms. Not a very satisfying mix, to be sure—many observers at the time and since, for example, squirm to contemplate the great African American activist Frederick Douglass consorting with the worst kind of partisan hacks as a Stalwart in the closing decades of the nineteenth century. But at least these hacks were willing to buy and sell votes to black people that their opponents would—and did—hang from trees.

3. Godkin quoted in Michael Harwood, "Chester Alan Arthur," in *The American Heritage Book of the Presidents and Famous Americans*, Vol. 7 (New York: Dell, 1969), 567.

4. Arthur quoted in Karabell, 53.
5. Karabell, 59.
6. Another widely quoted remark, this one can be found in Harwood, 569, and as the opening line of Karabell's biography.
7. Mark O. Hatfield with the Senate Historical Office, *Vice Presidents of the United States, 1789–1993* (Washington: U.S. Government Printing Office, 1997), 251–256, accessed at http://www.senate.gov.

## CHAPTER FIVE

1. Quotes and details of this incident come from Edmund Morris, *The Rise of Theodore Roosevelt* (1979; New York: The Modern Library, 2001), 144.
2. Morris, *Rise of Theodore Roosevelt*, 149.
3. Roosevelt quoted in Wilson Sullivan, "Theodore Roosevelt," in *The American Heritage Book of the Presidents and Famous Americans*, Vol. 8 (New York: Dell, 1969), 663.
4. Sullivan, 670.
5. Sullivan, 664.
6. Hanna quoted in Sullivan, 665.
7. The term "progressive" is lower-case here to distinguish it from the Progressive (or "Bull Moose) political organization founded by Roosevelt himself in 1912—a point at which the movement had become the dominant force in American politics and the dominant chord in Roosevelt's own political ideology.
8. Edmund Morris, *Theodore Rex* (New York: Random House, 2001), 54. Capturing the full complexity of Roosevelt's racial views is difficult even in a full-scale biography, much less a brief sketch. An avowed elitist and imperialist, it's hard to know whether to wince or laugh when TR describes his "hearty admiration for the Japanese" and other "Asiatics" while explaining why he considers their mingling with Americans on the West Coast to be undesirable, or as he castigates American women for their failure to reproduce as quickly as those of other races. (A life-long supporter of suffrage, TR believed American women needed to be smart and strong mothers of American men, gamely allowing for those freaks of nature who turned out to be chemists or novelists.) Such opinions of course were hardly unique at the time, but Roosevelt had a way of propounding them that could make him sound ridiculous even to his contemporaries. Yet it's also worth

emphasizing that TR was among those who stressed environmental, rather than genetic explanations for racial difference: Inferiority was a matter of nurture, not nature, and he had every expectation that "dusky" races could and would catch up. He viewed Booker T. Washington as a prime specimen in this regard, and, by the admittedly lame standard of American presidents, comes off pretty well—much better for sure than his Democratic successor, the avowed segregationist Woodrow Wilson.

9.  Theodore Roosevelt, "First Annual Message to Congress," December 3, 1901, at "The American Presidency Project": http://www.presidency.ucsb.edu.

10. Morris, *Theodore Rex*, 89.

11. This exchange is reported in Morris, *Theodore Rex*, 91–92.

12. Roosevelt quoted in Morris, *Theodore Rex*, 316.

13. Morris, *Theodore Rex*, 165–166.

14. Theodore Roosevelt, *An Autobiography* (1913; New York: Da Capo, 1985), 485.

15. http://www.theodoreroosevelt.org/life/timeline.htm.

16. Kathleen Dalton, *Theodore Roosevelt: A Strenuous Life* (New York: Knopf, 2002), 3.

## CHAPTER SIX

1.  The Federal Emergency Relief Administration (FERA) gave small grants or loans to the indigent; the Civilian Conservation Corps (CCC) provided jobs for young people in government-owned properties like national parks; the Public Works Administration (PWA) undertook construction projects like sidewalks and post offices. Some alphabet agencies worked under the aegis of the National Recovery Administration (NRA), established by the NIRA; others fell under the supervision of the Agricultural Adjustment Administration, created by the Agricultural Adjustment Act of 1935.

2.  Franklin Delano Roosevelt, "Speech at Madison Square Garden," October 31, 1936, http://history.acusd.edu/gen/text/us/fdr1936.html.

3.  This was a common expression of pleasure at a positive outcome at the time. For one version of FDR's use of the phrase in the context of the court-packing fight, see syndicated columnist Joseph Alsop and Turner Catledge's article of September 18, 1937, available at http://www.restoreliberty.com/9-18-37a.html.

4.  Frankfurter and Garner quoted in Conrad Black, *Franklin Delano Roosevelt: Champion of Freedom* (New York: Public Affairs Books, 2003), 413; 417.

5.  It would be tempting to argue that Roosevelt's polio—or, as a 2003 peer-reviewed medical study now indicates, Guillain-Barré syndrome—was a turning point in the making of his character. But this does not seem to be the case. Certainly, an illness of the kind he sustained (in 1921, when he was 39 years old) would leave its mark on anyone, and it's hard to believe that the tragedy that befell this golden boy would not chasten him and ground him. But in many fundamental respects, FDR was the same man: He was a slightly devious figure with his mentor, Navy secretary Josephus Daniels, before he fell ill, and a slightly devious figure with his ally, New York governor Al Smith, after he fell ill. He had a strained partnership with his wife before he got sick, and that partnership got reaffirmed while remaining strained as Eleanor stood by him ever after. The same goes for his more attractive qualities as well: his charm, his optimism, and his unshakeable confidence remained fixtures of his personality, their power impressive less because they were augmented than because they survived intact. When, on his first day back at his law offices, Roosevelt fell and sprawled across a marble floor, he laughed and reassured onlookers. He called out to two young men and a chauffeur to give him a hand, gripped his crutches with white knuckles, and said, "Let's go!" Convinced of the therapeutic power of hydrotherapy in Warm Springs, Georgia, he bought an entire resort and opened it up to fellow polio victims, regardless of their ability to pay. When confronted with a problem, he addressed it with cheerful pragmatism—truly a gift for himself and others.

6.  FDR, "Speech at Chicago, Illinois" (also known as the "Quarantine the Aggressors" speech) in *The Essential Franklin Delano Roosevelt*, edited by John Gabriel Hunt (Avenel, NJ: Portland House, 1995), 143.

7.  FDR, press conference, December 17, 1940, in Franklin Delano Roosevelt, *Great Speeches*, edited by John Grafton (New York: Dover, 1999), 80.

8.  These were the days in which the United States was still a major oil exporter; it was during the Second World War that the vast reserves of Arabia were discovered. On his way back from Yalta in 1945, Roosevelt stopped in Arabia and established ties with the

Saud royal family, resulting in one of the great fortunes—and problematic diplomatic relationships—of modern times.

## CHAPTER SEVEN

1.  The ensuing account of Johnson's strategy in the 1948 Senate race draws heavily on the reporting of Robert Caro in *The Years of Lyndon Johnson: Means of Ascent* (1990; New York: Vintage, 1991), esp. 369–372.
2.  Appointed, naturally, by Johnson by 1965. But his proposed appointment as chief justice in 1968 was filibustered by Republicans—in part because of his relationship with Johnson—and Fortas retired from the court entirely the following year.
3.  Caro, *Means of Ascent*, 399.
4.  Caro, *Means of Ascent*, 356.
5.  "Kennedy was pathetic as a congressman and as a senator," Johnson said in some taped notes to himself in 1969. "All of us have squealers after us—the girls who giggle and the people who are just happy to be with you. But Kennedy was the only one the press saw fit to report on."
6.  The Kennedy administration had begun wiretapping King at the insistence of FBI director J. Edgar Hoover, who detested King. When Robert Kennedy had questioned the necessity or propriety of the move, Hoover essentially blackmailed the brothers, showing them he had compromising information on them. Johnson needed no such convincing, and indeed routinely gathered information on those he considered opponents throughout his presidency. The practice continued under Richard Nixon—and, while unconfirmed, is almost certainly going on today.
7.  Nick Kotz, *Judgment Days: Lyndon Baines Johnson, Martin Luther King, and the Laws That Changed America* (Boston: Houghton Mifflin, 2005), 314. Wallace lived until 1998, having repented his segregationist ways.
8.  The text can be accessed in its entirety at The History Place Great Speeches Collection: http://www.historyplace.com/speeches/johnson.htm.
9.  Caro, *Means of Ascent*, xxi.
10. For one such citation, see http://www.southernstudies.org/news/fs20040826.htm. Johnson's prescience extended beyond Civil Rights. "Don't pay any attention to what those little shits on the campuses do," he said of Vietnam protesters to under-secretary of

state George Ball in 1965. "The great beast is the reactionary elements in the country. Those are the people we have to fear." See Robert Dallek, *Lyndon B. Johnson: Portrait of a President* (New York: Oxford University Press, 2004), 221–222.

## CHAPTER EIGHT

1. Haig's query and the subsequent dialogue draws principally from the research and interviews of Ford adviser James Cannon, in *Time and Chance: Gerald Ford's Appointment with History* (1994; Ann Arbor: University of Michigan Press, 1998), 292–294.
2. Cannon, 249.
3. Ford quoted in Peter N. Carroll, *It Seemed Like Nothing Happened: America in the Seventies* (1982; New Brunswick, NJ: Rutgers University Press, 1990), 153.
4. Some writers have speculated that the circumstances of Ford's childhood—as a young adult he played peacemaker between his mother and biological father, who failed to pay child support—help explain his actions as president. They may have also played a role in his willingness to marry Betty Warren, a divorcee. This was a relatively unusual decision for a young bachelor in the Midwest, and an indication of Ford's independence of mind and perhaps his decency (though he delayed the wedding until after a congressional election to avoid political controversy). The Fords would have four children. Betty Ford, who sometimes felt neglected by her husband, had a lifelong struggle with alcoholism. Her candor on this subject as well as about breast cancer—again, at a time when such subjects were avoided—made her an admired and even beloved figure.
5. For this well-known slam and other examples of Johnson's wit, see the web page devoted to the subject: http://www.working-humor.com/quotes/lyndon_johnson.shtml.
6. In an act of typical good sportsmanship, Ford taped an appearance for *Saturday Night Live* later in his presidency.
7. The Democrat, Carl Elliot, is quoted in Cannon, 70.
8. Cannon, 299; 307.
9. Cannon, 338; 348; John Robert Greene, *The Presidency of Gerald R. Ford* (Lawrence: University Press of Kansas, 1995), 17.
10. Barry Werth, *31 Days: The Crisis that Gave Us the Government We Have Today* (New York: Nan A/ Talese/Doubleday, 2006), 221.
11. Gerald R. Ford, *A Time to Heal* (New York: Harper & Row, 1979), 158–60.

12.  Cannon, 374–376.
13.  This phrase comes from Lincoln's famous address at Cooper Union (1860), suggesting Ford's awareness of history.
14.  The speech can be accessed in its entirety at the website sponsored by the Gerald R. Ford Presidential Library and Museum: http://www.ford.utexas.edu/library/speeches/740060.htm.
15.  Cannon, 384–385.
16.  Rodino quoted in Cannon, 389.
17.  On the evening of his first day in office, Ford met alone with Secretary of State Henry Kissinger and told him that he was considering an announcement that he would not run for president in 1976. He had made such a statement during his Senate confirmation hearings for the vice presidency, and such an announcement now, he thought, would strengthen the perception of his commitment to governance rather than politics. The ever-calculating Kissinger pointed out that such a move would likely hurt rather than help Ford's effectiveness, since he would be perceived as a lame duck without effective power. Ford took Kissinger's advice, and, of course, ended up running for reelection. But this incident is one more indication of Ford's almost touching innocence (or, alternately, evidence of his lack of fitness for anything other than a caretaking presidency). See Werth, *31 Days*, 27.

## CHAPTER NINE

1.  "Iran-Contra Hearings; The Testimony: A Defense Secretary Left Largely in the Dark," *The New York Times*, August 1, 1987, Section 1, p. 5. Accessed at nytimes.com.
2.  Douglas Kneeland, "Disgrace Charged," *The New York Times*, October 22, 1980; Bernard Gwertzman, "Confusion over Iran; *The New York Times*, November 20, 1986, A13. Accessed at nytimes.com.
    There are assertions, never proven, that Reagan campaign operatives, notably future CIA director Robert Casey, had been secretly in touch with the Iranian government prior to his election, promising arms to Iran in exchange for keeping the hostages longer so as to embarrass President Carter and improve their own electoral prospects—the so-called October Surprise, a phrase which has become synonymous with late-election-cycle drama.
3.  Larry Rohter, "Sandinistas Pin Hopes on Congress," *The New York Times*, March 3, 1985, Section 4, p. 1. Accessed via nytimes.com.

4.  For this and other widely circulated examples of Reagan's sense of humor, see http://politicalhumor.about.com/cs/quotethis/a/reaganquotes.htm.

5.  Reagan's March 4, 1987, speech is available at http://www.presidentreagan.info/speeches/iran_contra.cfm.

6.  Schroeder explains the origins of the phrase in making eggs for her children in *24 Years of House Work and Still a Mess* (Kansas City: Andrews McMeel Publishing, 1999), 91.

7.  Garry Wills, *Reagan's America: Innocents at Home* (1987; New York: Penguin, 2000), 9.

8.  By many accounts—some of them from his own offspring—Reagan left a lot to be desired as a parent. Perhaps the most bizarre illustration of this shortcoming occurred when he was governor of California and the guest of honor at a local high school, where he was commencement speaker. Afterward, he posed for a picture with the new graduates, and worked the event like any politician in that situation would, introducing himself to strangers. "Hi, my name's Ronald Reagan. What's yours?" he asked one new graduate. That graduate replied, "Dad, it's *me*. Your son. Mike." Edmund Morris reports this anecdote from an interview with Michael Reagan in *Dutch: A Memoir of Ronald Reagan* (New York: Random House, 1999), 318.

9.  http://www.c-span.org/classroom/govt/1980.asp.

10. Peggy Noonan, *When Character Was King: A Story of Ronald Reagan* (New York: Simon & Schuster, 2002), 186. There's a slightly more graphic version of Reagan struggling to breathe in Morris, *Dutch*, 431.

11. Reagan's speech is available at http://www.americanrhetoric.com/speeches/ronaldreaganevilempire.htm.

12. "Reagan Said to Joke in Speech of Bombing Russia Before Radio Speech," *The New York Times*, August 13, 1984, A16. The paper reported that in October of 1982, Reagan had made a similar gaffe in a voice test, describing the Polish military government as "a bunch of no-good lousy bums."

13. Gorbachev said this to Morris. See *Dutch*, 556.

14. Among other places, the dialogue between Reagan and his advisers is quoted in Michael Schaller, *Reckoning with Reagan: America and Its President in the 1980s* (New York: Oxford University Press, 1992), 173. Even Reagan's critics sometimes pondered whether his robotic demeanor really reflected reality. In one classic *Saturday Night Live* sketch from the late 1980s, cast member Phil

Hartman plays Reagan giving a notably idiotic photo opportunity. Yet once the camera is off his expression changes sharply and he barks a series of orders that suggests he's a hands-on boss from hell. As with his predecessor, Dwight Eisenhower, historians have revised their view of Reagan to suggest a much more engaged figure than public perception would allow. In particular, Reagan came to his views by deeply engaged reading and note-taking; however simplistic or even incorrect such views may have been, he was no mere mouthpiece for the interests he represented.

15. Dinesh D'Souza, *Ronald Reagan: How an Ordinary Man Became an Extraordinary Leader* (New York: Touchstone, 1999), 185, 192.

16. Joel Brinkley, "Reagan Takes a Poke at Gorbachev on Nicaragua," *The New York Times*, December 2, 1987, A10. Accessed via nytimes.com.

17. http://archives.cnn.com/2001/US/11/06/gen.attack.on.terror.

18. A transcription as well as videotaped version of Ron Reagan's eulogy for his father can be found at http://www.americanrhetoric.com/speeches/ronreaganeulogyfordad.htm.

## CHAPTER TEN

1. *The Starr Report: The Independent Counsel's Complete Report to Congress on the Investigation of President Clinton* (New York: Pocket Books, 1998), 75.

2. Clinton made this pledge during his acceptance speech at the Democratic Convention on July 16, 1992. It is available at the American Presidency Project: http://www.presidency.ucsb.edu.

3. Clinton quoted in John Harris, *The Survivor: Bill Clinton in the White House* (New York: Random House, 2005), 5.

4. Bill Clinton, State of the Union Address, January 25, 1994, at the American Presidency Project: http://www.presidency.ucsb.edu.

5. David Gergen, *Eyewitness to Power: The Essence of Leadership, Nixon to Clinton* (New York: Simon & Schuster, 2001), 308; Harris, *The Survivor*, 115–116.

6. In 1997, Clinton did sign the Children's Health Initiative Program (CHIP), a bill sponsored by Democrat Edward Kennedy of Massachusetts and Republican Nancy Kassebaum of Kansas. It provided insurance coverage to millions of children, the first major expansion of government into health care since the passage of Medicaid in 1965.

7. Newt Gingrich, *To Renew America* (New York: HarperCollins, 1995), 99.
8. Branch quoted in Harris, *The Survivor*, 159.
9. Clinton, State of the Union Address, January 24, 1995, at the American Presidency Project: http://www.presidency.ucsb.edu.
10. Most observers agree that Clinton's finesse on welfare reform was brilliant politics. But was it brilliant policy? The jury is still out on that. Welfare rolls have dropped precipitously in the last decade. What's unclear is whether this is the result of a generally strong economy, an effectively reformed system, or recipients on the old AFDC model not applying for benefits they may in fact still be eligible to receive.
11. The ensuing exchanges are recorded in David Maraniss and Michael Weisskopf, *Tell Newt to Shut Up: Prize-Winning Washington Post Journalists Reveal How Reality Gagged the Gingrich Revolution* (New York: Simon & Schuster, 2001), 147–148.
12. Of course, neither Mrs. Armey or anyone else in his immediate family held policy-making posts anything like Mrs. Clinton's in health care. Armey and Hillary Clinton had an edgy exchange in 1994 when she was presenting the administration's health care plan to Congress. Armey had opened a hearing with her by promising to make their conversation "as exciting as possible."

    "I'm sure you will do that," she replied.

    "We'll do the best we can," Armey said.

    "You and Dr. Kevorkian," she countered, to laughter. (Kevorkian was a controversial Michigan attorney who performed assisted suicides.)

    "I've been told about your charm and wit, and let me say the reports on your charm are overstated and the reports on your wit are understated," Armey retorted. In the end, of course, Armey would have the last laugh when the Clinton plan was derailed. See Harris, *The Survivor*, 115.
13. Maraniss and Weisskopf, *Tell Newt to Shut Up*, 148.
14. Gingrich quoted in Harris, *The Survivor*, 217.
15. George Stephanopoulos revealed that this was a scripted line in *All Too Human: A Political Education* (1999; Boston: Back Bay Books, 2000), 405.
16. By pushing Congress to pass a series of tax increases, Lyndon Johnson was able to leave office in 1969 with a small budget surplus.

## EPILOGUE

1.  The logic of the Munich analogy remained part of American foreign policy and played a major role in formulating the case for a war in Iraq. See Thomas E. Ricks, *Fiasco: The American Military Adventure in Iraq* (New York: The Penguin Press, 2006), 16–17.

2.  C. Vann Woodward, "*Strange Career* Critics: Long May They Persevere," *Journal of American History* (December, 1988): 862. Woodward's essay was part of a forum on *The Strange Career of Jim Crow* (New York: Oxford University Press, 1955), his classic work of race-relations that itself became a document, even instrument, of the Civil Rights movement.

3.  Information on the war on Iraq came from contemporary news accounts\ Ricks's *Fiasco*, Michael R. Gordon and General Bernard E. Trainor, *Cobra II: The Inside Story of the Invasion and Occupation of Iraq* (New York: Pantheon, 2006), and Bob Woodward, *State of Denial: Bush at War, Part III* (New York: Simon & Schuster, 2006).

4.  Perhaps the best recent account of the disaster is Douglas Brinkley, *The Great Deluge: Hurricane Katrina, New Orleans, and the Mississippi Gulf Coast* (New York: Morrow, 2006).

5.  This discourse about U.S. fiscal policy has been relatively quiet, steady, and marked by a barely suppressed sense of dread. One of the more informed and vivid discussions can be found in Kevin Phillips, *American Theocracy: The Peril and Politics of Radical Religion, Oil, and Borrowed Money in the 21st Century* (New York: Viking, 2006).

6.  For a revealing exploration of the complexities of Washington the slaveholder, see Henry Wiencek's brilliant *An Imperfect God: George Washington, His Slaves, and the Creation of America* (New York: Farrar, Straus and Giroux, 2003). That George Washington was deeply implicated in an evil system is beyond doubt. That he understood this, and sought, ultimately successfully, to extricate both himself and his slaves from that system is something that Wiencek also makes clear—and in so doing illuminates yet another way, at a time we're prone to forget, why George Washington was truly an impressive man.

## AFTERWORD

1.  Henry David Thoreau, "Slavery in Massachusetts," at http://www.sacred-texts.com/phi/thoreau/slavery.txt.

2.  In the first chapter of *Walden*, "Economy," Thoreau jokingly noted that his bill for "washing and mending, which for the most part were done out of the house," has not been received. That's because his laundry was done by his mother and sister, who did not charge him for this little piece of outsourced labor. See http://www.kenkifer.com/Thoreau/economy4.htm.

# SOURCE NOTES

ome time in the middle of 1969, when I was six years old and making the transition from a rented row-house apartment in Queens, New York, to a rented apartment in suburban Port Washington, New York, my mother's best friend at the time, Dorothy O'Dea, gave me a twelve-volume set of *The American Heritage Book of the Presidents and Famous Americans* (New York, Dell, 1968). Richard Nixon had just been elected to office, and an insert on his new administration was tucked into the final volume. The gift was an act of extravagant generosity, not least because it overestimated my reading comprehension ability by about a decade and a half. Even so, the lavishly illustrated volumes, studded with short sidebars, became a reliable standby when I had time on my hands or a term paper to write. The set has followed me wherever I have lived in the almost forty years since, and it is no exaggeration to say that without those books this one never would have been written. I thus begin this bibliographic essay by expressing gratitude to the editors of American Heritage not simply for this particular work, but for a truly marvelous mid-century publishing operation that, in its accessibility and confidence, shaped a generation of boys (and, I imagine, a clutch of plucky girls willing to overlook the unconscious sexism that marked so much writing of the era). The happy memories I and others have of this work sustain us in what is now a more self-aware, but perhaps more brittle, time.

A much more modern resource was also instrumental in this book, more so than others I have written: the Internet. The World Wide Web has, of course, been with us for well over a decade now, but its reliability as a source of information has been (and in many ways remains) shaky. Still, in writing this book, I have found it wonderful—literally a source of wonder—that I could, say, come across a reference to a letter James Madison wrote to Thomas Jefferson in a book I was reading, go online, and, thanks to websites like www.constitution.org, download and print the text in full within minutes. Federal government resources like the Library of Congress "American Memory" collections (www.memory.loc.gov/ammem) or www.senate.gov have been invaluable. And while some have raised questions about its veracity, I have also drawn upon the collective resources of what may truly be termed the peoples' work, Wikipedia (www.wikipedia.org). As has always been true, such sources should be used with care and corroboration, as should any number of reference works one can find at a local library. But the Internet in particular makes it possible for those of us without university appointments, travel grants, and access to archives to write do-it-yourself history.

This brings us to the point in notes like these where the author makes a now-clichéd observation about standing on the shoulders of giants. Actually, in my case, it would be less accurate to say that I stand on such shoulders than that I merely peep over them. No self-respecting academic historian would consider this a "real" work of history: I uncover no previously unknown facts, make no unique interpretive revision, or even situate myself in any specific subdisciplinary discourse. I have also gone light on the footnotes, generally limiting them to direct quotations from my sources or to add contextual information. Many of the quotations here will be familiar to anyone who has studied the figure in question; some will be easily accessed with a search engine such as Google. *Imperfect Presidents* is not a monograph or a survey, but more a collection of essays patterned on the work of Richard Hoftstadter's classic *The American Political Tradition and the Men Who Made It* (New York: Knopf, 1948). I would never contend this book approaches the greatness of that one. But if nothing else, I believe my role models are well worth emulating in matters of clarity, style, and their commitment to the sustaining myth of the general reader, on whom democracy itself is said to depend.

In that spirit, the notes that follow are not comprehensive of all the sources consulted, but instead list some of the important works that helped me and would help anyone else who seeks to understand the presidents in question. This bibliographic essay is self-consciously a snapshot of a moment, a survey of the historiographic landscape of an era (generally defined here as about a quarter-century). The emphasis is on recent and Amazon.com-friendly sources a reader might seek as a starting point. My fond hope, of course, is that the end for me will be a beginning for you.

GEORGE WASHINGTON. The most important modern biographer of Washington is James Thomas Flexner, whose four-volume study was published by Little, Brown: *The Forge of Experience, 1732–1775* (1965); *George Washington in the American Revolution, 1775–1783* (1968); *George Washington and the New Nation, 1783–1793* (1970); and *Anguish and Farewell, 1793–1799* (1972). The four volumes have been usefully abridged into a single book, *George Washington: The Indispensable Man* (1974). Other more recent biographies include John Ferling, *The First of Men: A Life of George Washington* (Knoxville: University of Tennessee Press, 1988); Richard Brookhiser, *Founding Father: Rediscovering George Washington* (New York: The Free Press, 1996); and Joseph Ellis, *His Excellency: George Washington* (New York: Knopf, 2004). Though not directly relevant, I'd like to put in a word for Henry Wiencek's *An Imperfect God: George Washington, His Slaves, and the Creation of America* (New York: Farrar, Straus, Giroux 2003), which usefully illuminates Washington's essential character. My primary source for passages quoted here is the 1997 edition of *George Washington: Writings*, edited by John Rhodehamel, part of the beautifully published series from the Library of America.

The Newburgh Conspiracy is a subject that is generally only treated in passing in biographies of Washington—and in those of one of the principal figures in the movement, Alexander Hamilton. I have relied heavily on the work of Richard Kohn. See in particular "The Inside History of the Newburgh Conspiracy: America and the Coup d'Etat," *William and Mary Quarterly* 27:2 (April 1970). Kohn also discusses the Newburgh Conspiracy in *Eagle and Sword: The Beginnings of the American Military Establishment* (1975; New York: Free Press, 1985). Kohn believes Horatio Gates was deeply involved in the Newburgh Conspiracy, though this has been contested. For one such view, see Paul David Nelson, "Horatio Gates at Newburgh: A Misunderstood Role," *William and Mary Quarterly* 29:1 (January 1972). Richard Brookhiser gives the affair all of a paragraph in his *Alexander Hamilton, American* (New York: The Free Press, 1999), perhaps because it puts this man he regards as a hero in a good deal less than a heroic light. Ron Chernow also tends to downplay any questions of treachery in his magisterial biography *Alexander Hamilton* (New York: The Penguin Press, 2004). As far as I could tell, the subject was entirely avoided in the ambitious Hamilton exhibition that ran at the New York Historical Society in 2004-05, perhaps because Brookhiser was one of the exhibition's advisers. For the relevant documents by Hamilton himself, see

*Hamilton: Writings*, ed. by Joanne B. Freeman (New York: Library of America, 2001).

THOMAS JEFFERSON. This is the place where one is supposed to talk about the sheer volume of Jefferson literature, fill an entire library, blah blah blah. In previous generations, one would routinely cite the gargantuan talents of writers such as Dumas Malone or Merrill Peterson, and anyone with a serious interest in Jefferson would do well to make a visit to such relatively distant country. Actually, some of the best recent work on Jefferson has not come from writers who have devoted their careers to Jefferson but instead have focused on aspects of his life. Of these historians, among them Garry Wills, first among equals is Joseph Ellis. In *American Sphinx: The Character of Thomas Jefferson* (1996; New York: Vintage, 1998), Ellis takes snapshots of different moments in Jefferson's career, a pioneering approach to the subject. Although not a primary focus, Jefferson looms large in *Founding Brothers: The Revolutionary Generation* (2000; New York: Vintage, 2002).

The papers of Jefferson himself run dozens of volumes under the editorship of Julian P. Boyd, et al. and published by Princeton. For decades now, Merrill Peterson's 1977 edition of *The Portable Thomas Jefferson*, part of the venerable series of "portables" published by Viking, has been the definitive one-volume abridgment. As far as the celebrated Adams-Jefferson dialogue goes, the indispensable source is Lester Cappon, *The Adams-Jefferson Letters: The Complete Correspondence Between Thomas Jefferson and Abigail and John Adams* (1959; Chapel Hill: University of North Carolina Press, 1988).

The Louisiana Purchase is a topic that has been widely written about, particularly around the time of its centennial in 1903 and the bicentennial in 2003. Probably the best recent study, both in range and depth, is Jon Kukla's *A Wilderness So Immense: The Louisiana Purchase and the Destiny of America* (New York: Knopf, 2003). I also benefited from pop historian Thomas Fleming's streamlined *The Louisiana Purchase* (Hoboken: John Wiley & Sons, 2003), part of an abortive but compelling "Turning Points" series (it appears to have lost out to the exceptional Oxford University Press series with a similar approach).

JOHN QUINCY ADAMS. The primary commentator on John Quincy Adams was JQA himself, whose dairy, as noted, was voluminous. A twelve-volume set—abridged—was edited by JQA's son, Charles Francis Adams (himself a distinguished diplomat and U.S. ambassador to England during the Civil War). There is, however, a nice single-volume edition edited by the great popular historian Allen Nevins (New York: Longmans, Greens & Co., 1929).

There are two good recent biographies of JQA. The more substantial is Paul Nagle's *John Quincy Adams: A Public Life, a Private Life* (1997; Cambridge, MA: Harvard University Press, 1999). Robert Remini, a distinguished biographer of JQA's antagonist Andrew Jackson, has also written a concise little book on Adams, part of the "American Presidents" series edited by the eminent Arthur Schlesinger, Jr. (New York: Times Books, 2002).

On the titanic struggle over the gag rule, the most important source is William Lee Miller, *Arguing About Slavery: John Quincy Adams and the Great Battle in the United States Congress* (1995; New York: Vintage, 1998), 39. This magisterial work by a magisterial historian (actually, he was trained as an ethicist) is central to the discussion presented here.

ABRAHAM LINCOLN. Here we go again: when it comes to biographical attention, Lincoln outstrips even Jefferson. (I refer anyone interested in wading into this ocean to my chapter on Carl Sandburg's epic biography, which surveys Lincoln biography generally, in Jim Cullen, *The Civil War in Popular Culture: A Reusable Past* [Washington, D.C.: Smithsonian Institution Press, 1995]). For contemporary readers, the one-stop-shopping biography is David Donald, *Lincoln* (New York: Simon & Schuster, 1995). Donald, professor emeritus at Harvard, is the former student of James Randall, whose multivolume biography of Lincoln set the academic standard for much of the twentieth century. Donald writes with exceptional authority and clarity.

As far as primary sources go, the definitive source has long been editor Roy P. Basler's *Collected Works of Abraham Lincoln*, first published in 1953 and reprinted by Rutgers University Press in 1990. Happily, however, the entire multivolume project is available online at www.hti.umich.edu/l/lincoln. You can't beat that for a comprehensive reference source. I will say, however, that the two-volume collection of Lincoln writings published by the Library of America in 1989 is a (compact) treasure that will grace any library. A one-volume paperback abridgment with an introduction by Gore Vidal was copublished with Vintage Books in 1992.

A select few books were instrumental in augmenting some of the issues discussed in this chapter in particular. A half-century after he began writing about the subject, Henry Jaffa's *Crisis of the House Divided: An Interpretation of the Issues in Lincoln-Douglas Debates* (1959;

University of Chicago Press, 1982) remains the definitive take on the subject and a work that belongs on the shortest of shelves devoted to Lincoln. William Lee Miller, who did such a marvelous job with JQA in *Arguing About Slavery*, brilliantly illuminates the moral dimensions of the Railsplitter's world in *Lincoln's Virtues: An Ethical Biography* (New York: Knopf, 2002). I was also greatly aided in grappling with the religious dimensions of Lincoln's thought by Allen C. Guelzo, *Abraham Lincoln: Redeemer President* (1999; Grand Rapids, MI: William B. Eerdmans Publishing Co., 2003). Four important works published while I was working on this one also served as a helpful backdrop: Joshua Wolf Shenk, *Lincoln's Melancholy: How Depression Challenged a President and Fueled His Greatness* (Boston: Houghton Mifflin, 2005); Doris Kearns Goodwin, *Team of Rivals: The Political Genius of Abraham Lincoln* (New York: Simon & Schuster, 2005); Richard Carwardine, *Abraham Lincoln: A Life of Purpose and Power* (New York: Knopf, 2006); and Thomas E. Schneider, *Lincoln's Defense of Politics: The Public Man and His Opponents in the Crisis over Slavery* (Columbia: University of Missouri Press, 2006). Schneider's book was particularly helpful in shaping my thinking on the issues I discuss in the Afterword of this book.

CHESTER ALAN ARTHUR. We're not drowning in sources here. In fact, Arthur has had only one major biographer: Thomas Reeves, *Gentleman Boss: The Life of Chester Alan Arthur* (New York: Knopf, 1975; a second edition was published by American Political Biography Press in 1991). Fortunately, it's a very good book. It was also fortunate for me that Zachary Karabell's short bio of Arthur, part of Arthur Schlesinger's "The American Presidents Series" (Times Books, 2004) came out in time for me to use it. The inspiration for this chapter, however, came out of left field. I resolved to include Arthur in here after reading Sarah Vowell's entertaining *Assassination Vacation* (New York: Simon & Schuster, 2005), which includes a shrewd and amusing take on the death of James Garfield and Arthur's succession to the presidency. History, to be sure, is far too important to be left to the historians.

THEODORE ROOSEVELT. Presidents like Thomas Jefferson and Abraham Lincoln have resulted in the leveling of entire forests, but with the exception of Jefferson's 1785 *Notes on the States of Virginia* (which, in truth, is lacking in narrative energy and even literary coherence), neither ever wrote a full-length book. Theodore Roosevelt, by contrast, was a prolific author. Though *The Naval War of 1812* (1882) was influential, and *The Winning of the West* (four volumes,

1889–1896) was quite popular, relatively little of his vast output has proven durable or relevant. One document that does bear reading, however, are his memoirs, *Theodore Roosevelt: An Autobiography* (1913; New York: Da Capo, 1985), which were published immediately following the tempestuous 1912 election. His speeches and essays have been widely anthologized; perhaps the best widely available concise edition is *Theodore Roosevelt: An American Mind*, edited with an introduction by Mario DiNunzio (New York: Penguin, 1994), which includes excerpts from his books.

Roosevelt's most prominent modern biographer is Edmund Morris. The first volume, *The Rise of Theodore Roosevelt* (1979; New York: Modern Library, 2001), won him the Pulitzer Prize and the right to author Ronald Reagan's authorized biography (more on this below). It is the source of the stories about Roosevelt's debut in the New York Assembly. The second volume of the Morris biography, *Theodore Rex* (New York: Random House, 2001), was the main account I used to render Roosevelt's role in the Northern Securities Case. The third volume, covering TR's post-presidential years, has not been published as of this writing. The best recent one-volume treatment is Kathleen Dalton, *Theodore Roosevelt: A Strenuous Life* (New York: Knopf 2002), a 25-year labor of love notable for its graceful prose and the critical scrutiny it brings to bear on its subject.

FRANKLIN DELANO ROOSEVELT. In contrast to TR and some of the other chief executives explored here, the writings of Franklin Roosevelt are scant and inaccessible. Surprisingly, I am aware of no anthology of his writings now available in print, though of course documents like his inaugural addresses may be accessed relatively easily online. My main print resource was *The Essential Franklin Delano Roosevelt*, edited with an introduction by John Gabriel Hunt (Avenel, NJ: Portland House, 1996).

Biographies of FDR, by contrast, are huge in number and size. So are more limited accounts of aspects of his life, like his relationship with his wife Eleanor or the coming (and decline) of the New Deal. Still widely read and admired after a half-century is James McGregor Burns, *Roosevelt: The Lion and the Fox* (New York: Harcourt, Brace & World, 1956). Kenneth Davis has written a multivolume Roosevelt biography; I found the fourth volume, *Into the Storm, 1937–40* (New York: Random House, 1993) useful on the court-packing controversy. Geoffrey Ward is another multivolume biographer; the volume I found particularly helpful is *A First-Class Temperament: The Emergence of*

*Franklin Roosevelt* (New York: Harper & Row, 1989). For a recent (albeit huge) one-volume biography written with opinionated verve, see Conrad Black, *Franklin Delano Roosevelt: Champion of Freedom* (New York: Public Affairs Books, 2003). Black, an alleged felon who ran his publishing empire into the ground, nevertheless knows how to write a good book. If you're looking for something concise, see the Roy Jenkins contribution to Arthur Schlesinger's "The American Presidents" series (Times Books, 2003).

LYNDON JOHNSON. Standing like a colossus over Johnson scholarship—standing like a colossus in the crowded field of presidential biography generally—is Robert Caro. Three of four projected volumes of "The Years of Lyndon Johnson" have been published by Random House. All three—*The Path to Power* (1982); *Means of Ascent* (1991); and *Master of the Senate* (2003) were instant classics. There's an obsessive, hypnotic intensity to Caro's work generally (he's also the author of a celebrated biography of Robert Moses—where, incidentally, one can learn a good deal about Franklin Roosevelt, among other figures). He ferrets out stories no one else has ever told, and a fiercely moral strain competes with utter fascination. A more measured take on Johnson comes from Robert Dallek, whose two-volume biography, *Lone Star Rising, 1908–1960* (1991) and *Flawed Giant, 1960–1973* (1998) have been combined in a shorter one-volume edition, *Portrait of a President* (2004), all published by Oxford University Press.

Less authoritative, but evocative and readable, is Doris Kearns Goodwin's first book, *Lyndon Johnson and the American Dream* (New York: Harper & Row, 1976). Goodwin worked for LBJ as a White House intern. Her husband wrote the address Johnson made to Congress promoting the Voting Rights Act.

Johnson on the page is like Johnson on television: bland and stilted. *A Time for Action: Selections from the Speeches and Writings of Lyndon Baines Johnson, 1953–64* (New York: Atheneum, 1964) is ponderous, while *Vantage Point: Perspectives on the Presidency* (New York: Holt Rinehart and Winston, 1971) is Exhibit A when illustrating the truism that presidential autobiographies are turgid and unrevealing. Fortunately, it is possible to gain a vivid glimpse of the man in action, thanks to the work of presidential historian Michael Beschloss. *Taking Charge: The White House Tapes, 1963–1964*, edited with commentary by Beschloss (New York: Simon & Schuster, 1997), captures the man in all his profane intensity, as does *Reaching for Glory: Lyndon Johnson's Secret White House Tapes, 1964–65* (New York: Simon & Schuster, 2001).

Johnson's complex relationship with Martin Luther King, a focus of this chapter, is discussed in depth in Nick Kotz, *Judgment Days: Lyndon Baines Johnson, Martin Luther King, and the Laws That Changed America* (Boston: Houghton Mifflin, 2005). The subject is also revealingly handled in the final two volumes of Taylor Branch's magnificent three-volume examination of "America in the King Years," published by Simon & Schuster: *Pillar of Fire, 1963–65* (1998) and *At Canaan's Edge, 1965–68* (2006).

GERALD FORD. A pair of books will give the reader a reasonably full account of Ford's life and times. James Cannon's *Life and Chance: Gerald Ford's Appointment with History* (1994; Ann Arbor: University of Michigan Press, 1988) is a sympathetic, sophisticated, and compelling biography by a former *Newsweek* editor and Ford aide. John Robert Greene's *The Presidency of Gerald Ford* (Lawrence: University of Kansas Press, 1995), part of an academic series on the presidency, offers a concise précis on the White House years. Bob Woodward and Carl Bernstein discuss Ford's situation as part of a larger story on the collapse of the Nixon presidency in *The Final Days* (New York: Simon and Schuster, 1976). This chapter benefited while I was drafting it from the publication of Barry Werth's *31 Days: The Crisis that Gave Us the Government We Have Today* (New York: Nan A. Talese/Doubleday, 2006), which zeroes in on the crucial weeks culminating in the pardon of Richard Nixon. Ford himself weighs in on the Nixon pardon and on the rest of his life in *A Time to Heal: The Autobiography of Gerald R. Ford* (New York: Harper & Row, 1979). The good-natured Ford is also the author of *Humor and the Presidency* (New York: Arbor House, 1987).

One final note. John Updike's 1992 novel *Memories of the Ford Administration* (reprinted by Ballentine Books in 1996) is a remarkably complex—and remarkably evocative—story that juxtaposes the presidencies of Ford and James Buchanan (of all people!) as a backdrop for a story about a junior college professor making his way through the sexual and family minefields of the mid-seventies.

RONALD REAGAN. The dean of Reagan studies—well, more like the journalist who was there at the creation—is Lou Cannon. *Governor Reagan* (New York: Putnam, 1982) and *President Reagan: The Role of a Lifetime* (New York: Simon & Schuster 1991) are essentially the first draft of Reagan's history. An updated and combined two-volume set was published by S&S as *A Life in Politics* in 2004. More interpretive is

Garry Wills now-classic *Reagan's America* (1987; New York: Penguin, 2000). Edmund Morris, the TR biographer chosen to be Reagan's authorized biographer, found himself paralyzed by writer's block before settling on the fictional device of writing as one of the people Reagan the lifeguard saved from drowning in *Dutch: A Memoir of Ronald Reagan* (New York: Random House, 1999). Though this approach muddies the factual veracity of the book, which was roundly criticized by reviewers, it is nevertheless a fascinating and revealing account of an exceptionally elusive figure. Robert Schaller's *Reckoning with Reagan: America and Its President in the 1980s* (New York: Oxford University Press, 1992) is a brief and largely critical overview. Much of the information I gleaned on the Iran-Contra Affair came from Jane Mayer and Doyle Mac-Manus, *Landslide: The Unmaking of the President, 1984–1988* (Boston: Houghton Mifflin, 1988).

Reagan's autobiography, *An American Life* (New York: Simon and Schuster, 1990) is a lifeless bore. But the publication of *Reagan, in His Own Hand: The Writings of Ronald Reagan That Reveal His Revolutionary Vision for America* (New York: The Free Press, 2001) generated much comment on publication because it belied the widespread perception of Reagan as a dimwitted puppet of his advisers. Such writings have led to a revisionist take on Reagan apparent in Kennedy and Johnson biographer Richard Reeves, who added Reagan to his portfolio with *Ronald Reagan: The Triumph of Imagination* (New York: Simon & Schuster, 2005). Historian Douglas Brinkley is editing the Reagan diaries, slated for publication in 2007.

BILL CLINTON. Two books by *Washington Post* reporters constitute what might be regarded as the semi-official record of Bill Clinton's career. David Maraniss' *First in His Class: The Biography of Bill Clinton* (New York: Simon & Schuster, 1995) traces Clinton's life from childhood to his decision to run for president. John Harris's *The Survivor: Bill Clinton in the White House* (New York: Random House, 2005) picks up the story with Clinton's inauguration. In between is the presidential campaign of 1992 itself, which perhaps is best captured by a novel: Joe Klein's 1996 *Primary Colors* (reprinted by Penguin in 1999), loosely patterned on Robert Penn Warren's 1948 novel *All the King's Men*. Klein, along with Marannis and Bob Woodward, have also written highly journalistic accounts of the Clinton years. See in particular Woodward's *The Agenda* (1994; New York: Pocket Books, 1995), which covers the tumultuous first year of the Clinton presidency.

Clinton himself weighed in with a doorstop of an autobiography, *My Life* (New York: Simon & Schuster, 2004). Other Clinton memoirs used here were Hillary Clinton, *Living History* (New York: Simon & Schuster, 2003), George Stephanopoulos, *All Too Human: A Political Education* (1999; Boston: Back Bay Books, 2000), and David Gergen, *Eyewitness to Power: The Essence of Leadership, Nixon to Clinton* (New York: Simon & Schuster, 2001).

# INDEX